More Praise for *Mastering the New Media Landscape*

"*Mastering the New Media Landscape* is an incredibly smart and informative work. If you are aiming to broaden your influence, start here—it will change the way you influence others for years to come!"
—**Tom Rath, #1 *New York Times* bestselling author of *StrengthsFinder 2.0* and *Are You Fully Charged?***

"Reading *Mastering the New Media Landscape* is a bit like having your two smartest friends take their time and patiently catch you up on everything that you've been missing. The online world has changed the media world, and it's not too late to catch up."
—**Seth Godin, author of *Purple Cow***

"Rusty and Barbara offer compelling, clear advice for approaching what seems to be an increasingly complicated media world. *Mastering the New Media Landscape* is an indispensable tool for anyone with a story to tell."
—**Andy Andrews, *New York Times* bestselling author of *The Noticer* and *The Traveler's Gift***

"In the old days, the only viable way to generate attention for you or your business was to buy it (advertising) or beg for it (traditional public relations). Today, this is how most organizations still attempt to get noticed. Barbara and Rusty show you a better way—understanding the world of micromedia where everyone is a publisher."
—**David Meerman Scott, bestselling author of ten books including *The New Rules of Marketing & PR*, now in 25 languages from Arabic to Vietnamese**

"The authors explain PR and media strategies to get attention you *own* rather than rent. It's a futureproof, long-term view of how to master new media views."
—**Ryan Holiday, author of *Trust Me, I'm Lying* and *Growth Hacker Marketing***

"In a fast-changing media milieu, this book provides a sure-footed blueprint for success."
—**Julie Silver, MD, award-winning author, successful entrepreneur, and Associate Chair for Strategic Initiatives, Department of Physical Medicine and Rehabilitation, Harvard Medical School**

"As a business practitioner, and having led an integrated communication company, I found the allocation of media budgets a major key to achieving success. The force of PR has been growing and growing. Now, PR skills play beautifully on the new media front. Social media and the new emerging micromedia have changed the communication landscape forever. I have seen Barbara Cave Henricks become a PR standout. Barbara and Rusty Shelton light up the complex, multifaceted, but oh-so-critical new media world. It's not just about being interesting—it's about the new way to get results."

—Peter Georgescu, Chairman Emeritus, Young & Rubicam

"If you want to grow your platform in today's media environment, this book is a must-read. Rusty and Barbara are truly two of the world's best when it comes to marketing and PR. Thankfully, they've created a go-to guide that walks you through each step of the process. Highly recommended!"

—Robert D. Smith, artist manager and author of *20,000 Days and Counting*

"This book provides an excellent, easy-to-understand framework for building your brand using fast-changing new media platforms."

—Jill Totenberg, CEO, The Totenberg Group

"The emergence of micromedia has changed the game for those promoting their company, products, or brand. With this brilliant new book, Barbara Cave Henricks and Rusty Shelton expertly explain how to navigate the new media rules and grow your audience from the ground up."

—Jackie Huba, author of three books on customer loyalty, including *Monster Loyalty*

"How to create the magnetic pull that builds your business! Put this book on *top* of your business reading list to learn how to show up humanly and authentically as the value-added thought leader. The way you communicate in the media world today is part of what compels people to want to be in touch and do business with you."

—Jeanne Bliss, author of *"I Love You More Than My Dog"* and cofounder of the Customer Experience Professionals Association

"The world of media is constantly changing, and Rusty and Barbara are on the forefront of it all. This book will help you stay relevant and knowledgeable about the future. It may help you stay in business."

—Rory Vaden, cofounder of Southwestern Consulting and *New York Times* bestselling author of *Take the Stairs*

"Read this book. It holds the precious gift of both context and clarity in an ever re-interpreted world of media."

—Charlotte Beers, former Chairman and CEO, Ogilvy & Mather Worldwide, and former Under Secretary of State for Public Diplomacy and Public Affairs

"This book is a vitamin-packed feast for anyone who's serious about building a brand or promoting a cause. You want to be discoverable? This book shows you how. You want to create an army of engaged followers? This is your guide. You want to get maximum impact from earned media, rented media, and owned media? This is your instruction manual. *Mastering the New Media Landscape* is not just a book title. It's what people who want to make a difference must be busy *doing*."

—Rodger Dean Duncan, bestselling author of *Change-Friendly Leadership*

"Two of the best media minds today have created a simple, elegant model for the new micromedia world. Beyond concept, Barbara and Rusty show us how to utilize tested strategies for building and strengthening our own media platforms rather than depending on the elusive dictates of the traditional gatekeepers."

—Ray Bard, Publisher, Bard Press, publisher of *The One Thing*

"Having an important message means nothing if nobody notices or cares. If you want to grow your audience in today's distracted and overcrowded world, read this book. Rusty and Barbara show you how to fascinate your audience."

—Sally Hogshead, *New York Times* bestselling author and creator of the Fascinate System

"Anyone wanting to get a message out into the world will benefit enormously from reading Barbara and Rusty's book. Fast-moving and engaging, it provides tons of insight into what's happening today in publicity and marketing and how to take best advantage of all the possibilities available in this new media world."

—Erika Andersen, founder of Proteus, business thinker, and author of the new book *Be Bad First*

"The best way for businesses and individuals to learn how to successfully promote their products and ideas is to be educated by pragmatists who are engaged in the process every day. Barbara and Rusty have written a wonderful and extremely useful book on how to deal with the three dimensions of micromedia—earned, rented, and owned. They explain how to leverage each dimension to gain the best return."

—Bill Davidow, Silicon Valley pioneer and author of *Overconnected*

"Barbara and Rusty have written a treasure map to a bestseller. Study it. Follow it. Then watch your book soar!"

—Jill Griffin, author at Harvard's *Working Knowledge* and author of *Earn Your Seat on a Corporate Board*

"The challenge facing us all is this: how do we stand out and stay relevant in the mostly disruptive and massively distracting world of micromedia? *Mastering the New Media Landscape* gives you the answers."

—Matthew E. May, author of *The Laws of Subtraction*

"For authors, what was once coasting down a smooth path is now riding a dirt bike over thousands of rocks and around a few hundred trees to hit the right jumps. Barbara and Rusty have ridden ahead to keep you from flying over the handlebars."

—Rodd Wagner, *New York Times* bestselling author of *Widgets*

MASTERING
THE NEW MEDIA
LANDSCAPE

Embrace the Micromedia Mindset

BARBARA CAVE HENRICKS

RUSTY SHELTON

BK
Berrett–Koehler Publishers, Inc.
a BK Business book

Berrett-Koehler Publishers, Inc.
1333 Broadway, Suite 1000
Oakland, CA 94612-1921
Tel: (510) 817-2277   Fax: (510) 817-2278   www.bkconnection.com

Ordering Information

Quantity sales. Special discounts are available on quantity purchases by corporations, associations, and others. For details, contact the "Special Sales Department" at the Berrett-Koehler address above.

Individual sales. Berrett-Koehler publications are available through most bookstores. They can also be ordered directly from Berrett-Koehler:
Tel: (800) 929-2929; Fax: (802) 864-7626; www.bkconnection.com

Orders for college textbook/course adoption use. Please contact Berrett-Koehler:
Tel: (800) 929-2929; Fax: (802) 864-7626.

Orders by U.S. trade bookstores and wholesalers. Please contact
Ingram Publisher Services, Tel: (800) 509-4887; Fax: (800) 838-1149;
E-mail: customer.service@ingrampublisherservices.com; or visit
www.ingrampublisherservices.com.

Berrett-Koehler and the BK logo are registered trademarks of Berrett-Koehler Publishers, Inc.

Printed in the United States of America

Berrett-Koehler books are printed on long-lasting acid-free paper. When it is available, we choose paper that has been manufactured by environmentally responsible processes. These may include using trees grown in sustainable forests, incorporating recycled paper, minimizing chlorine in bleaching, or recycling the energy produced at the paper mill.

Production Management: Michael Bass Associates
Cover Design: Bradford Foltz, Image by Corbis
Author Photos: Rusty: Katrina Barber, Barbara: Ashley M. Stroud Photography

Library of Congress Cataloging-in-Publication Data
Names: Henricks, Barbara Cave, author. | Shelton, Rusty, author.
Title: Mastering the new media landscape : embrace the micromedia mindset / Barbara Cave Henricks, Rusty Shelton.
Description: First edition. | Oakland, CA : Berrett-Koehler Publishers, Inc., [2015] | Includes bibliographical references and index.
Identifiers: LCCN 2015041814 | ISBN 9781626565807 (pbk.)
Subjects: LCSH: Internet in public relations. | Internet marketing. | Digital media. | Information technology—Social aspects.
Classification: LCC HD59 .H436 2015 | DDC 658.8/72—dc23
LC record available at http://lccn.loc.gov/2015041814

First Edition
20 19 18 17 16 15   10 9 8 7 6 5 4 3 2 1

C58872
JL

Barbara Cave Henricks

For my husband, Michael McDougal,
who has given me a book-worthy happy ending,
and my children, Kate, Corey, and Brady,
the communicators of tomorrow

Rusty Shelton

For the love of my life, my wife Paige;
our boys, Luke and Brady; and our new baby girl
for inspiring me every day.
And for my parents, Walt and Roxanne,
and sister Courtney, for the love and support
I've been so blessed to receive through the years.

CONTENTS

INTRODUCTION

BE HONEST: What was the first thing you did when you woke up this morning? Before your feet hit the floor, did you roll over and check your smartphone? If you are like most of us, you did a quick scan within the first minutes of waking. And the habit didn't stop there. In fact, there is a fire hose of information that follows you into your day, with media hitting you from all directions. From the TV you click on at breakfast to the Periscope feed you watched as you polished off your coffee, from the radio button you hit in the car to the podcast you switched to when the commercials started, from the newspaper you scanned when you arrived at the office to the blogs you read when you opened your email, you are living in a brand-new media landscape. Although the specific media each of us consume will be different, the universal truth is we are more connected to information, and each other, than ever before.

As we sit down to write this book, we are acutely aware of just how fast the world is changing. We know that content will always exist, but how it will be consumed is anyone's guess. You may be reading this from a physical book, on an e-reader, or via an app on your smartphone. Certainly more devices and apps are just ahead. Even less clear is where you will hear about the content you consume in a media landscape that has been completely transformed in the span of two decades. This book is our attempt to examine the sweeping changes in the media, explain their impact, offer insight, and suggest a strategy for you to not only tackle the change but conquer the new, expansive environment before us.

To many of us, the new media environment feels like the Wild West. On television, many of today's highest-rated programs are reality based and feature families who do things like procreate excessively or leap to fame when their patriarch pops into view as part of the legal team for O. J. Simpson. Even talent shows, popular since Ed Sullivan introduced the world to the Beatles, have given way to celebrity-judged singing duels where tone-deaf contestants appear to try out but, in fact, are merely being mocked. Twitter helped Paris Hilton, a descendant of the famed hotelier, become well known. After a sex tape brought her to public notice, she became a devoted user of the clever communication tool, employing it to do nothing but advance her own fame.

And let's not leave out the whole concept of going viral, such as the frenzy that erupted in 2015 over whether a particular dress was blue and black or white and gold. That gem of a story seized so much attention that real news was pushed, at least briefly, from the headlines. It's easy to be cynical. We get it.

But, let's flip the tables for a moment. Today's media environment has given us access we wouldn't otherwise have to many of the world's most influential minds. Seth Godin was a very successful book packager more than two decades ago, turning out superior books and running his startup from a tiny Manhattan apartment. After selling that company to employees and launching two technology companies, he began a career as an author, gave birth to the concept of permission marketing, and has arguably become the most iconic marketing expert of his time. With dozens of books to his credit and perennial bestsellers like *Tribes, Linchpin,* and *Purple Cow,* what does Godin use to remain in the public eye?

Largely, a blog that he began in 2002 and uses to dispense advice as well as road-test ideas for new books.

A blog may or may not be the right tool for you, but the lesson here is that in the new media landscape, anyone now has the ability to build an audience if they approach it in the right way.

But it wasn't always like this.

Before the enormous disruption largely created by technology, the media landscape was dominated by what we now think of as traditional or legacy media. These large national media companies were the gatekeepers who determined which stories received coverage, with an eye toward the material most relevant to their readers, listeners, or viewers. The decisions about what was newsworthy were made in newsrooms, editorial meetings, and under the watchful eye of an editor or producer who had ultimate veto power. Traditional media relied on the expertise of a large group of trained communicators.

Then, between 2000 and 2008, one in four media jobs disappeared. While that statistic came from a Forrester Research study conducted even *before* the financial crash of 2008, those of us who work with the media every day already knew it. Local media shrunk dramatically, while the big national outlets became understaffed and under pressure to create content not only for their regular beats or programs, but for their online presence as well. Meantime, we began to witness the birth of a new kind of media—digital outlets hosted by individuals and brands that feature blogs, podcasts, webinars, and other content tailored to a very specific group of readers. We call these micromedia, and collectively they are creating a new way to get attention for your platform, your message, your mission, your story, or your business.

You may be wondering: what is micromedia?

Everyone. Literally every individual, business, and organization is a micromedia outlet, whether they know it or not.

Everyone with a smartphone can be one part camera operator, one part humor columnist, one part radio host, or whatever kind of media outlet they would like to be.

This isn't anything new.

We have always had the human impulse to gather and share information, making us micromedia outlets, in a sense, even before the Internet or social media came along and gave us an amplifier. Before technology gave us new tools for sharing, most of us influenced two groups of people: those in our direct physical space and the friends and family members we kept in our circle with letters, phone calls, and visits. Those who wrote for a church newsletter or sent out a yearly holiday update to their "list" might have influenced more people in that environment, but for the most part, we had to go to a lot of dinner parties to be a true influencer.

Fast-forward to today—there are still some micromedia who primarily influence in "pre-Internet" ways (physical environment/friends and family), but the vast majority of micromedia are now influencing exponentially more people than ever via the Internet. Some micromedia have grown their audience so large that they rival traditional media in terms of reach while others influence several hundred via Facebook, Instagram, or Twitter.

Both matter tremendously to anyone looking to get a message out.

Part of the reason many micromedia outlets are doing so well is that they are challenging the status quo and removing the traditional gatekeepers. They are amassing their own sizeable audiences and beginning to play a much larger role in influencing public opinion. As the power and reach of traditional media continue to erode, many of the big players are looking to these new, smaller outlets as the best option for future growth. Others are re-forming and forging alliances with one-time competitors in an effort to strengthen their diminishing brands. The twenty-first century has already seen the creation of *Bloomberg Businessweek*, *Newsweek*/The Daily Beast (2010–2013), and Disney/ABC Television (purchased by Disney in 1996). Furthermore, AT&T acquired DirecTV; Altice, a French company, acquired Suddenlink; and Comcast made a prolonged but ultimately failed effort to acquire Time Warner Cable—all further evidence that mergers among the traditional giants, which are struggling to survive, will continue as the millennium moves on.

Consumers began to really feel the shift in the mid-1990s when online-only, general interest publications such as Salon.com (1995) and Slate.com (1996) became among the first to dip their toes into the fast-moving water. They were swiftly joined by dozens and then hundreds of other online-only publications whose combined cachet and clout now arguably comes close to commanding the attention once reserved for the evening network news or the newspapers plucked daily from the porch or newsstand. In an op-ed in the *New York Times*, author and NPR host Kurt Andersen aptly describes the 1990s as the era in which the digital age got fully underway. "At the beginning of the decade, almost none of us had heard of the web, and we didn't have browsers, search engines, digital cellphone networks, fully 3-D games, or affordable and powerful laptops. By the end of the decade, we had them all."[1]

Although the changes in media started almost two decades ago, many marketers, branding experts, authors, small business owners, entrepreneurs, nonprofit organizations, and activists are still operating as if they remain in a media environment where top-down messaging is the only way to grow support for ideas, products, and services. As a result:

- Major companies around the world are spending billions of dollars on PR and marketing processes that are not suited for this new environment.

- Individuals looking to grow their own platform focus far too much attention and resources strictly on traditional methods, missing huge opportunities to grow their own micromedia channels or use coverage in these channels to open the doors of the large, traditional outlets that remain.
- Small businesses, authors, and speakers are increasingly aware of social media options and tools, but few can grasp how to create the right strategy to grow their own micromedia audience.
- Marketers fail to recognize that often the best way to get major media attention is to first capture the attention of micromedia.
- The power of micromedia has been and continues to be vastly underestimated by nearly everyone who desperately wants to use it for forwarding their message.
- Millions are missing the opportunities that micromedia provides as both a forum for content and also a momentum generator.

Our theory is that the fallout will continue, that the millions of micromedia outlets not only will survive but will multiply, and the very noisy world in which we live will become flat-out deafening.

The seismic shift in how content is created, where it is housed, and who can create it has resulted in both an enormous challenge *and* a huge opportunity. Millions can now get their messages heard by micromedia, starting small, gaining traction, and then growing loud and large enough to command the attention of the traditional outlets whose impact remains important. The challenge of using micromedia for this purpose demands a dedicated willingness to participate. These new outlets possess a raging appetite for highly credible, quickly produced, quality content that will appeal to the audience they were designed to serve. This appetite means there are more outlets to run your content. This shift is enormous, given that even a decade ago being asked to contribute to an esteemed publication was a rare occurrence at best.

Micromedia offers another kind of opportunity for those eager to embrace its potential to become a thriving media outlet in their own right, growing an audience that they own the connection to. This set of brave and fledging digital journalists are aware that platforms like Twitter, Instagram, Tumblr, LinkedIn, and Facebook, to name just a few, give them the power to reach their audience in a new way. However, too many who want to become micromedia outlets lack the communication skills and editorial savvy needed to create a following. They are, by and large, not professional journalists and too often create a "me-first" platform. This is a treacherous and uphill battle—something we will explain in greater depth later in this book.

The rise of micromedia is stirring questions from two camps: those deeply willing and interested in using them as levers to gain coverage in traditional media, and those eager to become their own outlets. While they might not yet have the skill set to effectively use the tools that now exist, they are highly motivated to learn. Here's what we are hearing from this group:

- How do I create an audience for my message?
- What is the one media hit—online or traditional—that will be the tipping point for me in terms of mass exposure?
- What is the best way to integrate traditional and social media for a campaign with broad depth and reach?
- How do I build my own email list?
- How should I approach social media, and is it worth my time?
- Why should I focus on online results? Isn't national media attention the only way to move the needle?

- How do I coordinate my social media efforts and outreach with my traditional media?
- How does working on one impact the other?
- What is the relationship between traditional and micromedia?
- How do I build a platform?

The answers to many of these questions are changing daily, as the *New York Times* is no longer the single hit that matters. The media environment that brought you *Sesame Street* as a child, MTV as a teen, and *Saturday Night Live* when you arrived at college is changed forever; and the influence and growing power of micromedia are rewriting the rules on how to get noticed. The message is clear: learn the new rules or be left behind.

Micromedia is further fueled by the generation that is currently coming of age. Described interchangeably as "digital natives" (a term coined by researcher Marc Prensky) or Gen Y, this new demographic brings with it new demands. Thomas Koulopoulos and Dan Keldsen, in their book *The Gen Z Effect,* say, "These kids are not just digital natives, they are hyper-connected junkies whose expectations will radically change business forever."[2]

While the new generation may lead the charge, *everyone* who consumes media will continue to demand more, regardless of age. We all want more, better, faster content that is customized to our interests and needs. We're not married to a specific medium; instead we consume media via a multitude of devices, in a myriad of ways, and all at our own convenience. We devise our own menu of media, picking and choosing among the options and diminishing the editorial control once wielded by traditional media.

Consider the scenario in your own home. Does anyone rush to catch the 6 p.m. news? Do your teenagers fight to control the family television? No. Because that 6 p.m. news is available 24/7 on any one of a dozen channels, and kids stream their favorite shows on their computers or smartphones, perhaps in the family den if a family binge-watching session has been scheduled, but nearly as often, alone in a personal window of free time. Just as it is time to recognize those changes, it's time to accept the fact that things have changed in how the media gets and covers stories and begin making strategic decisions about how to capitalize on the new, exciting world before us.

The game is not only afoot—it is here. Who, at the end of the day, will curate the content that we consume? And if we are trying to crack into that content, how do we figure out which social media tools make sense, what strategy can be deployed to create media momentum once generated by local media that was severely decimated in the crash of 2008, and who among those trying to gain notice and grow a personal audience have the power, skill, and capacity to become a micromedia outlet in their own right? This book will examine these questions, offering a primer of the current media landscape and a guidebook of how to navigate it for marketers, branding experts, authors, small business owners, nonprofits, and entrepreneurs. Furthermore, it is our fondest hope that we can help you understand how to leverage the three categories that matter most today—rented, earned, and owned media—and that collectively position you to master the new media landscape.

1 WELCOME TO THE AGE OF MICROMEDIA

DO YOU HAVE WHAT IT TAKES to master the new media landscape?

Few are aware that they do have what it takes, and, in truth, we didn't either until we embraced a new approach that took us out of our comfort zone and into a brand new approach—a micromedia mindset.

In the coming pages, we're going to explore how we arrived at this new media landscape and what we can learn from lessons of the past as we plan for a future media environment none of us can possibly predict.

What's ironic is that we're not that far removed from a PR environment that, against the backdrop of Periscope and Instagram, feels like the stone age of communications.

We entered our careers in public relations a couple of decades apart. Rusty's first job out of college was with a book publicity agency in Austin, Texas, while Barbara left her editor's desk at NBC Radio in Washington to join Workman Publishing in Manhattan. Although the years we began our careers were 2004 and 1989, respectively, when we crossed paths in 2009, we quickly decided that our viewpoints, skill sets, and even the age gap contributed to making us ideal collaborators. We both had a solid foundation in public relations, but Rusty, a digital native, brought social media expertise and a skill for helping others understand it, while Barbara brought years of New York publishing experience and a journalist's eye for shaping content suitable for both traditional media and micromedia. Since joining forces, we have teamed up on scores of projects, from working with leading brands like IBM, Chicken Soup for the Soul, and Campbell Soup Company to grow their audiences, to launching bestsellers like *Strengths-Finder 2.0*, *The Confidence Code*, and *The One Thing*. We can confidently report that rather than sticking to our core capabilities, we've each created a company of professional communicators who can work across disciplines in today's complex media world.

We began like thousands of other publicists charged with setting up events and getting lots of earned media for every author on our list. We were each handed what was then considered the industry bible, *Bacon's Media Directories*, a set of dark green encyclopedic directories that housed "up-to-date" listings of the media, organized in volumes—one for newspapers, one for magazines, and a third for broadcast outlets. Three categories. That was it. They arrived *annually* via standard U.S. postal delivery in a bulky package and were the center of heated exchanges between publicists, as we raced to copy pages needed for each project before relinquishing them to the next person in line. Updates? We used Wite-Out to change contact info when producers, editors, or hosts changed jobs.

It was clearly not just a different era but a different lifetime in almost every way possible for those with a story to tell (and the marketers who help them tell it). In short, everything about the way promotion and marketing are handled has changed.

There have been many causes for these changes, but the chief disruptor has been the Internet, followed by social media, which have made us much more connected to one another (at least in a technological sense) and less connected to media conglomerates that used to dominate the airwaves.

If we look back at the media world of even ten years ago, major media outlets could be described as boulders, encircling the public. These boulders made decisions to let in whatever information they deemed worthy of consumption; and if a book, product, or message wasn't covered by "traditional" media, it was very difficult for us, the general public, to hear about.

Word of mouth existed, but it took a lot longer to take hold because it happened in physical proximity—dinner parties, places of worship, and the like—instead of via social networks that transcend physical connections.

Then came the Internet, followed closely by social media, which took a collective sledgehammer to those boulders, spreading pebbles across the ground and leaving those major media outlets casting a much smaller shadow over the public. As those pebbles scattered, so did our attention, fragmenting the way we consume media.

Thanks to our newfound access to high-quality, niche information, many of us now prefer to pay attention to the more specialized pebbles, which, while small, give us exactly what we want, as opposed to the "traditional" or "legacy" media outlets that often aren't able to—because of less local coverage and an increased reliance on wire services due to shrunken newsrooms.

Stone age analogies aside, the pebbles are still scattering, and they are forming a brand-new media environment.

Welcome to the age of micromedia.

HOW CAN YOU SUCCEED IN THIS ENVIRONMENT?

Success in this new age is largely about embracing a micromedia mindset. If you are open to a new way of thinking about the media environment, you have made the first step toward participating in it. The influence economy has truly arrived, but the main problem is that most are approaching promotion as if boulders of big media and its gatekeepers still ruled the day.

The new media landscape has three types of media—earned media, rented media, and owned media—and you must effectively leverage all three to be successful.

Earned media used to be the only game in town when it came to telling a story or marketing a product. We define earned media as any exposure you get by earning your way onto someone else's platform or stage. This could range from an NPR interview to an op-ed in the *New York Times* to an interview on Dave Ramsey's EntreLeadership podcast to a tweet from Guy Kawasaki. To obtain earned media, you need permission from whoever owns that platform to give you access to their stage, so to speak. When they do so, it's powerful because not only are you reaching that audience, but you have the implied endorsement of that media outlet as well. The challenge with earned media is that it is extremely difficult to get. You must go through whoever controls the outlet, and you are at the mercy of their decision. Your fate rests in the hands of the gatekeepers who control access to earned media, and it is hard work to capture their attention and ultimately gain access to their stage.

Rented media emerged as a sizeable space with the growth of social media. We define it as a presence and content that you control but that lives on someone else's platform or stage. Rented media includes *your* Facebook page, *your* Twitter account, *your* LinkedIn profile, *your* Instagram feed, and so forth. We overloaded that sentence with italics because you don't ultimately "own" those channels—you're creating and posting content on a little sliver of real estate owned by someone else. At any time, Facebook can tweak their algorithm, Twitter can shut down your account, LinkedIn can change its rules, and access to your audience on that platform can change forever. This doesn't mean rented media isn't incredibly important—we'll talk plenty about why it is crucial to your success—but it means that to master the new media landscape you can't be content leaving your audience on someone else's real estate.

The final category of media is owned media. Understanding and growing owned media is, in our minds, the crux of embracing the micromedia mindset and the key to mastering the new media landscape. We define owned media as any channel where you fully own the connection to your audience, including your website (assuming it lives on a domain you own), your blog (again, assuming it lives on a domain you own) and your email list. Growing an audience that you own gives you leverage when you have a story to tell, a product to sell, or a message that the world needs to hear. It also gives you the ability to shine a spotlight on others who don't yet have a platform but could benefit your audience.

Put simply, owned media equals ongoing value in this new environment, but utilizing all three kinds of media is a must for a fully integrated strategy. As the figure below shows, each category organically feeds the other but the key to growing your owned media audience is making sure you create a

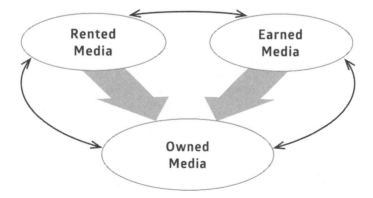

magnet (a call to action) to intentionally and consistently push audiences from earned and rented to owned space.

Each of these three, collectively, add up to define your platform or personal brand. Like nearly everything else in today's world, your platform will be customized based on your goals, passions, message, and audience.

Are you thinking across each of these buckets?

To succeed, a different approach is needed from both marketers, who should be working with their clients to help them grow their own micromedia platform, and individuals, businesses, and other entities who must embrace the opportunity in front of them to grow an audience that they own the connection to.

Some of you will say, "We have already changed; we're building meaningful relationships with bloggers and getting excellent coverage. We have a Twitter account and a Facebook page, and we're getting more active."

Those are good first steps, but it's not enough. It's time to stop chasing access to other people's platforms and take center stage on your own platform.

THINK LIKE A MEDIA OUTLET

We want you to think of your digital platform as if it is your personal media brand—your newspaper. We judge a media outlet by the value of its content and pay attention to those that entertain and inform us. We increasingly put our social media connections through the same filter we use for media based on the options we have (block, unfollow, mute, etc.). We all have friends, family, and other connections that we gloss over when scrolling our Twitter stream or Facebook newsfeed because we don't value their content. We lose interest for an infinite number of reasons that range from constant promotion to an endless stream of baby pictures or political diatribes.

At the same time, we pay particular attention to certain individuals or brands because their content informs and entertains us. We get value from their updates, and, in exchange, we give them something that truly matters in today's environment: our attention.

In this age of micromedia, it doesn't take much for us to change the channel. Because we have more options, we expect more than ever from those we pay attention to. One bad post, one off-target tweet, or one too many promotions and attention wanes or, worse, disappears—often forever. The challenge before you in today's largely democratized space isn't getting attention—it's keeping it.

Think about what kind of newspaper you would value subscribing to. You almost certainly wouldn't subscribe to a newspaper filled with ads, selfies, or me-first content (okay, unless it was really funny or self-deprecating). You also likely wouldn't subscribe to a newspaper that is delivered without any consistency—once or twice a month just wouldn't cut it. We subscribe to newspapers that provide interesting and entertaining content on a consistent, predictable basis. Those that feature interviews, reviews, and other news we can use— the kind of information we can put into practice that day-to-day make our lives better. You are going to be judged by the same standard we apply to broader media.

FILL YOUR AUDITORIUM

If you are reading this book and want to grow your audience moving forward, it is time to take center stage.

As you get started growing your platform, imagine yourself taking the stage in a huge auditorium. Unless you are already famous or in some way well-known, you are going to be looking out from the stage at a very sparse crowd. Your initial audience will be gathered in the front couple of rows and will likely consist of friends and family there to support you as you launch your blog, podcast, or other content channel.

Before you say anything from the stage, it is important to remember that everything you do in this public arena will either help or hurt you in terms of growing the audience in your auditorium. In the digital environment, which is largely anonymous, people can get up and walk out as quickly as they came in, and they have zero qualms about doing so. If your blog doesn't cut it or you spend too much time "selling" from the stage, the only people left will be those who *can't* leave—good friends and family (and they're dozing off, rolling their eyes, or muting you).

On the other hand, if you are dynamic with your content and provide entertaining and informative information, you give your initial audience content they can share with their audiences (as micromedia outlets themselves, each of them have their own stage—even if they're just speaking to Facebook friends). When they share your blog post, they stand out in the hall with a big sign and point their audience into your auditorium.

Once their friends arrive, they will make a very quick decision on whether they want to sit down (by subscribing), stand in the back (just reading the post), or head on back out the door. Much of what they do will depend on a combination of the look and feel of the stage, which is the content on your website. Is it professional? Does it provide a clear overview of the value you will provide? Are you giving people a reason to sit down and subscribe via a quiz, free download, or other value proposition? Are you popular right now with the people sitting in the audience? Do they see a lot of commenting and sharing? The quality of the content you are providing from the stage of your website needs to engage, as most will want you to hook them quickly or they will be gone.

Although the audience is judging you on a number of things, they are also doing so very quickly. According to a study done by the Nielsen Norman Group, the longer you can keep someone in your auditorium (your website), the better chance you have that they will sit down:

It's clear from the figure below that the *first 10 seconds of the page visit are critical* for users' decision to stay or leave. The probability of leaving is very high during these first few seconds because users are extremely skeptical, having suffered countless poorly designed Web pages in the past. People know that most Web pages are useless, and they behave accordingly to avoid wasting more time than absolutely necessary on bad pages.

If the web page survives this first—extremely harsh—ten-second judgment, users will look around a bit. However, they're still highly likely to leave during the subsequent twenty seconds of their visit. Only after people have stayed on a page for about thirty seconds does the curve become relatively flat. People continue to leave every second, but at a

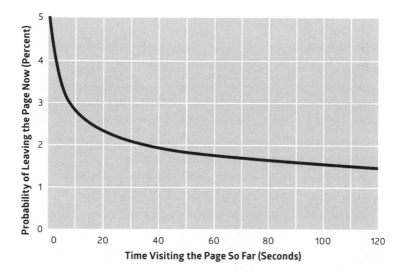

much slower rate than during the first thirty seconds. So, if you can convince users to stay on your page for half a minute, there's a fair chance that they'll stay much longer—often two minutes or more, which is an eternity on the Web.

The question you need to ask yourself is this: "Am I giving someone a good, clear reason to stay on my website/blog?" If not, the doors to your auditorium are revolving—you may get a number of people in, but they aren't sticking around.

We'll be discussing ways to fix that problem so you can own the connection to your audience. We will also explore at length how to get people through the doors of your auditorium by building relationships with individual influencers and groups, and effectively using rented and earned media.

Although traditional or earned media, as we will be calling it, is changing, based on syndication, influence, and scarcity, we believe it is more powerful than ever in terms of getting a message out. So while we want you spending plenty of time in your auditorium creating content, interacting with others, and building an audience, we're also going to challenge you to devote more effort to acquire earned media coverage as well by getting on larger stages that you don't own.

The key change we want to encourage you to make is to think of reaching an audience via earned or rented media, not just as the end goal but rather as crucial components of driving people to your owned media space, be it your website or email list, where you can extend that interaction for a much longer period of time. In the age of micromedia, every interview, speech, guest post, and other public event is not only an opportunity to reach those people during that short interaction, but also an opportunity to then give them a reason to head to your website and convert to your platform.

In the coming pages, we will explore numerous case studies of how to do this, ranging from the authors of the runaway bestseller *The Confidence Code*, Katty Kay and Claire Shipman, who grew a huge email list by pairing a clear call to action with a national media campaign to drive more than 150,000 people to their website to take their free confidence quiz; to bestselling author and speaker Jon Acuff, who leveraged in-person meet-ups in cities where he was already traveling to build relationships that gave him the ability to make the most important career transition of his life. You will also hear from experts such as Fred Allen of *Forbes* and Patricia O'Connell, a former editor at *BusinessWeek,* on how to craft great content and what it takes to be a contributor.

Even though we will discuss it at length, this is not a book about social media.

Despite the amount of time we'll spend looking at how to get great media attention, this is not a book about PR.

Although we'll walk through case studies of speakers who have built massive audiences through in-person events, this is not a book about driving attention via events.

Rather, this is a book about a new kind of mindset that all who have a story to tell in today's modern media environment need to embrace—before the window of opportunity disappears.

Not only does growing a large, owned media audience give you leverage to share your own ideas, but it also allows you to grow meaningful relationships that can change lives. The key is to think more like a media executive than a marketer. The most important opportunity is not the short-term sale; it's getting someone to take a seat in your auditorium.

Let's get started.

2 TECHNOLOGY GIVES RISE TO NEW RULES OF COMMUNICATION

TOM RATH IS A STATISTICIAN AT HEART. Someone who, despite the break-out success of books like *StrengthsFinder 2.0*, and *How Full Is Your Bucket?*, remains a well-mannered Midwesterner who prefers to fly under the radar and could live happily off the grid. So imagine our trepidation when, at long last, we convinced him to do some desk-side briefings in New York, and Tom's sense of polite protocol and technology went head-to-head.

Barbara was gleefully shuttling Tom to media appointments when the unthinkable happened during a lunchtime chat with a reporter from *Fortune*. Unable to simply turn off her smartphone lest a journalist need to reach her and shuffle the day's schedule, Barbara found herself staring at Tom's mortified face when the phone's insistent vibrating began to make the tabletop quiver. A quick glance at the screen revealed a local area code, so Barbara stepped into the hallway to attend to what seemed quite likely to be a schedule change or other piece of crucial information. The call? It was a recorded voicemail from her Manhattan hotel informing her that the time of turn-down service had been changed and would now commence at 8 p.m., rather than 9 p.m. Fortunately, Tom is a forgiving soul, but this is all too familiar a scene in our world where the rules of good communication—some might even say basic manners—seem to have been turned on their head.

Smartphone blunders are the least of it. In a recent piece in the *New York Times,* reporter Judith Newman explored what she called the new horrors that accompany every new piece of technology.[1] Specifically, she details the anxiety, fear, and straight-up gaffes that happen when the auto-fill feature of email does its alleged magic. Auto-fill is that handy tool that aptly fills in names and other information in a field based on a few keystrokes. Its sister, auto-correct, does this as well, but it goes past corrections and *predicts* what you are writing in the body of the note. These features are great when they keep you from looking up someone's email address for the tenth time or when you get a little dim on that spelling lesson about "a lot" always being two words. Much less so when they insert your mother's name rather than your best friend's in the address box of an email. Even worse is when they transform someone's name in the *body* of a note into a word that's a bit off-color or flat-out obscene. "Secrets are disclosed, petty true feelings are revealed, words (and worse, photos) of longing and lust end up in the box of your boss instead of your lover," Newman writes. "And no one is immune."

COMMUNICATION IN THE VIRTUAL WORLD

The collective effect of technology's ever-growing sophistication means millions now have democratic access to public platforms and can create a groundswell of interest without the invitation or permission of traditional media gatekeepers. The power once held by a select few has begun a definite and seismic shift to the individual. It also demands mastery of a new way to communicate. Adopt a micromedia mindset, one that accommodates the needs of this new landscape, and go forth with confidence.

Here are some guidelines and suggestions to keep close at hand when crafting your messages and making your first forays into the newly expanded public stage.

Never sacrifice credibility

As you build your strategy and adopt a micromedia mindset, whether with the goal of using coverage as leverage to crack into traditional, earned media space or with the hopes of becoming a micromedia outlet yourself, remember that the single-most important factor in content creation is objectivity. Be clear, be informative, be entertaining, but always be objective. It is the golden rule of journalism but a rule that, if adopted by those in the micromedia world, will help us maintain the integrity of content that made those traditional outlets revered.

Consume online media to familiarize yourself with what they offer

Whether you have carefully tended your social media accounts for years or are just getting started, changes in content, format, and focus happen very quickly online. Start with the outlets that you already read or that personally interest you. Navigate through them carefully to see what kind of material they are featuring (guest blog posts, reviews of services or products, interviews with experts) and where you might fit into their editorial plan. Next, add sites (start with five to ten) with an audience that mirrors the one you'd like to capture. In both cases, you are laying the groundwork for a successful strategy in the new media landscape.

Blogs, podcasts, video segments, and social media forums such as Facebook, Twitter, Tumblr, LinkedIn, Instagram, and Snapchat feature material that follows their own specific rules. Learn what is expected and appropriate before you participate or lobby for coverage. Ask for coverage in specific columns, feature stories, reviews, or other ways that make sense for that particular outlet. If they feature bylines, by all means ask for one. If they do interviews with business leaders, offer yourself up for a spot there. Pleas of "Cover my new book," "This would make a great story," or "Attached please find an op-ed" should only be made when you are certain the outlet is in search of content in that format or for a specific area of its publication or site. Make it clear you know what kind of content that outlet features, and let its owner know how you can participate with that unique format in mind.

Create content for the niche, not the general audience

As the media landscape has stretched and expanded to the online space, the focus of the content has shifted. Rather than appealing to the masses, much of the online material you consume was created for a very specific niche audience. This narrowing of interest was clearly made possible by the larger space available to house it. The new, expansive environment is comprised of a seemingly endless number of media outlets with tight, specific focus. Today, audiences flock to customized content the same way they fill the aisles of every Starbucks store in search of a cup of coffee made specifically to suit them. The one-size-fits-all mindset that drove our economy for decades has been swiftly replaced by an environment in which consumer demand for customized offerings is vital to commercial success.

Create your content with this in mind. Don't strive to appeal to "everyone" because that audience has dispersed. Stop homogenizing your messages so that they are palatable, or at least understandable, to the masses. The masses have moved on. The mass has fractured back into individuals who now each have the power to customize and consume their own content stream. Find your ideal audience, your perfect customer, and write or create material especially for them.

Value the niche audience

We speak every day to those in search of media coverage. And time and again, we hear what we consider to be both an arrogant notion and a fateful mistake. While media wish lists are likely to feature dream targets with national scope and enormous reach, too many people consider niche or trade industry outlets with disdain. With the excuse that these publications or outlets are "too small to matter" or "I can always get coverage there without any effort," far too many march past their natural first audience—the one *most* likely to become rabid fans eager to tell everyone that your content is genius.

Those with small followings may count among their audience the exact people who need your information most. As for not needing to try *at all* to be featured on a site aimed at a very specific niche audience, we would contend that this is very unlikely. Precious few of us have been pursued by a media outlet convinced that our insight, material, or contribution are invaluable to their site or success. Start with the base that will be most interested in your message, garner coverage and support from those outlets, and use it to persuade larger outlets that your story has the potential to pique the interest of a bigger, perhaps more general, audience.

Carefully monitor your contributions

Once you have found a home for your content in the micromedia world, do not assume that your job is over. In fact, consider the public forum just the first step on your path to widespread attention. Once you have put a public stake in the ground and are offering up your ideas to the masses, be certain to listen, very carefully, to the feedback and conversations that take root around your ideas.

Set up a system to monitor everything you release. Every comment, tweet, retweet, favorite, or like is an important piece of data that will guide you to the ideas and subjects that are most resonant and most likely to be fertile ground for expansion. Just as you archive that content on your own site, on your hard drive, to the cloud, and hopefully to a USB as well, learn to listen closely and carefully to what your audience is saying. Be open to cheerleaders and critics alike, as both will inspire you to expand your thoughts and your contributions.

Foster relationships with your followers and your dream followers

Once you are listening to your audience, make the effort to forge a meaningful connection with them. Read the comments beneath that blog post and respond. Take the time to create a list of those tweeting or retweeting your content, research their profiles, and add them to your own outreach pile. Take all of this a large step forward by beginning to consume content from those in your audience. It may turn out that the VP of Marketing who is commenting on your LinkedIn post is creating crazy-good material herself. Sign up for that feed. Comment on her post when it has special resonance. And don't stop there.

Turn your attention next to those who you *wish* were reading, listening, or watching you. First, consume their material. Take to the online stage to comment on it *only* when it truly sparks an interest and a response that moves the conversation forward. This is definitely a case where false, empty flattery will get you nowhere. What's more, it will be viewed as an opportunistic ploy to claw your way into notice and, ultimately, good favor. Let authentic interest guide you, and set your sights on being useful rather than self-promotional. Used well, this kind of dogged focus on those in the circle you wish to enter will end with the target becoming intrigued with the thoughtful responses and, perhaps when the time is exactly right, becoming interested in what else you might have to say.

Done poorly, it means you will be put in the spam filter for the rest of time.

What the new rules really mean

In total, these new rules for communicating are meant as a quick refresher course for anyone participating in the micromedia world. They are designed to remind us all that while the social media tools and spaces before us give us the opportunity to do new, different, visual, and interactive things with our audience, they are best used by a practiced hand. Don't let the speed of the new environment rush you into communicating in a way that lacks polish and professionalism. Fast is good, but only if you can achieve it while staying true to your image and your brand. Take an extra minute when composing that next tweet, posting a blog, or even replying to someone who comments on your work. That time won't be wasted, and soon it will become a good, solid communication habit.

3 UNDERSTANDING THE OPPORTUNITIES IN MICROMEDIA

IN THE FALL OF 2014, Andrew Edgecliffe-Johnson wrote a tremendous article in the *Financial Times* titled "The Invasion of Corporate News" that explored the disappearing chasm between journalism and PR, writing, "The lines between journalism and PR are rapidly becoming blurred as business interests bypass traditional media to get their message across."[1] He cites the growing number of companies, including Chevron, GE, Wells Fargo, Target, and others, that have created micromedia channels to provide entertaining and informative information that (they hope) their fans want to read and share. The goals of this new breed of corporate communications are no different from major media outlets: they want to create content that their audience is seeking so they can grow their influence. Journalists do this via news and companies, and individuals can now do it by telling stories about their products and services in compelling ways.

As part of the piece, Edgecliffe-Johnson interviewed Ashley Brown, who built Coca-Cola's content marketing program before joining Austin-based Spredfast. She said, "If they can produce content that is sufficiently emotionally engaging and useful, fans will share it on social media. We advise customers that the world needs more great content." Edgecliffe-Johnson continues, "But broadcasters and magazines no longer have a lock on distributing compelling stories: individual consumers are just as likely to do the job for brands."

He's right, of course—and this shift isn't just happening in the news business. Groups that have had a lock on distribution for decades, from record companies to book publishers, are now fighting for survival, racing to innovate and change, as their business models face disruption from all sides.

We could have a spirited discussion on whether the democratization of distribution is, in general, good or bad for consumers (most would argue that it is good), but one thing is certain when it comes to the changes in the media landscape: they provide an enormous opportunity for those individuals and brands that are willing to become content creators themselves.

THE OPPORTUNITY OF MICROMEDIA

Jon Acuff is a face-to-face kind of guy.

Nevertheless, he's built a huge social media platform, including a successful blog and hundreds of thousands of social media followers, and has written several *New York Times* bestselling books, including his latest, *Do Over: Rescue Monday, Reinvent Your Work and Never Get Stuck.* He gives speeches on numerous topics, including the power of social media, reminding audiences "communities make the world (and ideas) go round." But what makes Jon different is that he has a passion for keeping face-to-face contact as an important part of his strategy at a time when so many others are making the shift to virtual communication for the lion's share of their audience-building work.

When you hear about community building in today's media environment, most people immediately think of social media, but the reality is that communities are built in a number of different ways. For example, if you ask Jon how he created such a huge online community, he'll point to the offline, in-person meet-ups he has done throughout his career as a big part of it.

Jon is on the road much of each year speaking in front of thousands of people. But unlike most others, when he goes to a city for a speech, he often sets up a separate, stand-alone meet-up that is free and open to the public. In these sessions, he gives a short presentation, answers questions, and just generally gets to know attendees.

At the end of those talks, Jon opens the floor to the audience, passing the microphone around and urging others to share their "Do Over" stories, which are often inspired by the ideas found in Jon's most recent bestseller. At a Dallas event we attended, Jon gave the audience a full thirty minutes to talk about whatever they were working on. We heard about an attendee's new podcast, a blog they just started, a new curriculum they are trying at church, their struggle to lose weight, and more—whatever was important to them at that time. As each person spoke, we saw nods of agreement from the audience, as if others were identifying with the message. Following this thirty-minute audience share, Jon stood and signed more than 150 books, spending more than two hours speaking with each and every fan as the long line made its way to him.

When he left Half Price Books that night, he had inspired a room full of people, who now feel a larger connection to him, with many of them now ready to be fully engaged with his online community—and, just as important, each other.

Jon told us, "I do face-to-face interactions because despite the many wonders of online engagement, there are still tremendous gaps it creates between you and an audience. It's one thing to have someone retweet you—that's a very thin connection; it's another thing to have them come share the same space with you. I think that deepens relationships in a way that online simply can't."

Based on loyalty built through the deeper personal connection he fostered that night, those who attended are now more likely to engage with his blog posts or Instagram pictures, sharing them with their micromedia audience and helping Jon's content to self-propel online.

Although in-person engagement, whether via a speech or a meet-up like this, tends to drive more connection than almost anything else, it's not the same path for everyone.

So, where should you start?

A GOOD MICROMEDIA STRATEGY STARTS WITH CLEAR GOALS

Kevin Cashman is a longtime consultant and client whose last book, *The Pause Principle*, offered an informed perspective that speed has some serious downsides in life and career. He likes to say "slow down to go fast," meaning allow yourself time to decide on the best course of action, before you begin, so you can move swiftly in the right direction. That mindset is so important when it comes to growing your audience. Before you decide how to spend your time, you want to first get clear on what your goals are. Do you want to build a consultancy? Would you like to ramp up your speaking? Do you want to acquire a thousand new customers over the next three years? Are you hoping to raise awareness for an important cause or mission? Would you like to build an audience for a future book or product offering that you're not sure about right now?

In today's media environment, your ability to achieve any of these goals starts and ends with your ability to successfully engage with earned, rented, and owned media. But if you aren't clear on your goals, you may end up spending time in areas where you won't get a maximum return on your investment.

There are an endless number of options when it comes to growing your audience. We often see people either spread themselves too thin by trying to create a presence on every social network they can find or do exactly the opposite by focusing all of their efforts on the channel they know best (typically Facebook).

Both are big mistakes because neither is driven by the question you should be asking, which is, *Which channel provides the best intersection between my skills/passion and my audience's attention?* For many speakers, a podcast is the perfect intersection for them, as it highlights their audio gifts, the very attributes they are trying to sell. Another thought leader trying to score coverage in a well-read business publication may decide to focus on his writing, figuring that a well-crafted piece will further his skills and move him closer to landing a contributor's spot.

We've seen successful micromedia channels built across every single platform online, so don't feel pressure to follow the crowd down a certain road. There is no one answer or one way to gain widespread attention. The thing all success stories have in common is a singular focus on providing content of value to an audience in a consistent and unique way.

The right channel for you is one where your target audience is listening; your passions, interest, and skills are suited to that media outlet; and activity there will put you closer to your goal. Your success often depends on the ability to find just the right situation and pursue it with equal parts skill and persistence. Essentially, that means you will begin thinking like a media executive.

SUCCESS IN MICROMEDIA ISN'T JUST ABOUT SOCIAL MEDIA

The media space used to be divided into well-defined silos by format: radio, TV, newspapers, and magazines. As the Internet grew in reach and importance, online media was added to the list. Then, as social media exploded onto the scene, it was added into yet another category.

Who knows what new categories will come next in terms of media format, and we don't think it's productive to divide formats by technology or medium. Instead, we believe it is much more helpful to divide media into categories based on ownership.

As we mentioned in Chapter 1, today there are three categories you need to be aware of (see the table below): owned media (channels you own and fully control), rented media (your social media channels, which live on real estate owned by someone else), and earned media (channels others own and control that you must earn access to).

Owned media

Owned media includes all channels that you have created and fully control. You own your website (and the blog there if it lives on your URL). You own your email list and you fully control the content delivered and frequency with which it arrives. Outside of extraordinary circumstances or poor email list management, no one can rob you of that list, nor can they limit or constrict the way in which you distribute content or information to it.

In today's environment, it is increasingly important to own a vibrant and effective media channel in your website.

Owned	Rented	Earned
Website	Social media	Media exposure
Blog	Advertising	Speaking
Email list		Influencer mentions
Podcast		Events

Furthermore, you should channel the attention you receive from earned and rented media back to your own media (your auditorium).

Rented media

Many people are under the mistaken impression that they own their Facebook page, Twitter account, or Instagram feed, but the reality is that these are rented media channels. At any point Facebook can change its algorithm and limit your ability to reach your audience. At any point Twitter can receive a complaint and shut down your feed. When you are producing content on each of these channels, what you are really doing is standing in a very small section of their stage and, with their permission, reaching a subset of their audience that has indicated they are interested in what you have to say. This is really valuable for you and is definitely something we want you to keep doing, but you also need to know that you don't own this real estate, and you don't want your main micromedia channel to live on someone else's stage.

Instead, think about rented media as a way to access people in a very large auditorium and interact with them in an engaging way. The goal, though, isn't to only keep their attention there—it is to find creative ways to drive them into your auditorium to join your list.

Rented media also includes advertising, whether online or traditional.

Earned media

Earned media includes all channels owned by others, from NPR's airwaves to Lady Gaga's Twitter account to TED's stage, that you must earn, rather than buy, access to. It also includes live events where you have earned the right to speak from the stage, talk to fans at a book signing, or reach them through any other kind of forum. The great thing about earned media is that people understand there is a significant vetting process before you are invited on someone's stage. NPR is one of the hardest bookings in PR. Lady Gaga rarely highlights a book or product outside of her own. Getting an opportunity to speak at TED is among the toughest challenges out there. Thus, when you do get on stage, it gives a huge amount of credibility to you and your message, and people are much more likely to take action on your advice as a result.

Earned media also includes online bios and blogs for the company where you work. The reality is that for many of the people, the first result on a Google search for their name is their bio page on the company website. That's fine if you own the company, and it's also okay to have that company page as the first result for a time, but your goal should be to have the first result in a search for your name as real estate that *you* own.

RELYING TOO MUCH ON ANY ONE FORM OF MEDIA

We're going to explore each of these three categories in detail in the coming chapters because we believe all three are incredibly important to you, and you need to have a clear roadmap for how to use each. As a general rule, you want to move people from earned and rented media to owned media. When you are reaching an audience via earned or rented media, you don't ultimately control how long you get to reach that audience or how often your posts will show up.

Let's take a look at Facebook's 2013 algorithm change as an example. For years Facebook worked to court brands around the world to start fan pages on the popular social network. Through official brand pages, companies, celebrities, and other public entities could build an audience consisting of hundreds, thousands, or even millions of "likes" from fans. In allowing these brand pages, Facebook granted permission to each brand to set up shop on its stage—the largest in the world—and build their own section of the audience. This was seen as a huge boon for brands, and it was. But the wake-up call sounded for many in December 2013 when Facebook changed its News Feed algorithm, and the result was far less organic exposure for brands. According to an analysis of brand pages done by Ignite Social Media, in the week after the change was made, "organic reach and organic reach percentage [had] each declined by 44 percent on average, with some pages seeing declines as high as 88 percent."[2]

In a single big move, Facebook elbowed brands that had spent years building large audiences on the site away from prime real estate on its stage, removing access to a large percentage of the amassed audience. It was a reality check for a number of top brands that started to recognize the importance of owning the connection with their audience on their own real estate rather than leaving that audience in a place they didn't control in rented space.

It's important to understand that a heavy reliance on earned and rented media is a potential problem not just for brands but also for individuals.

This is a common misconception for those who believe it is okay to house their entire audience on someone else's real estate. For example, let's say you are a popular drive-time radio host in Houston, and you reach 75,000 people every weekday afternoon. That seems like an awesome platform, doesn't it? And it is—but the problem is that each time you're on the air, you're talking to an audience that you don't own, and you are doing it in someone else's auditorium. The ability to reach that audience daily is a great thing, but you must realize that every time you go on the air, you are on borrowed time. The moment that radio station sells to Clear Channel or your ratings slip and a syndicated show replaces you, you are pulled off the stage and sent back to your own auditorium. If you haven't been intentionally driving people to your auditorium, via real estate that you either rent (Twitter, Facebook, LinkedIn) or, even better, own, you have missed a huge opportunity. Once you are off the air of that Houston station, it may be hard for your audience to find you unless you created the path for them to follow while you still sat in that studio.

This same rule applies to thought leaders who blog for a top online publication like *Inc.*, *Fast Company*, the *Huffington Post*, or any other popular publication. It's awesome that you get to reach millions of people from Inc.com's stage, but you must be fully aware that you're speaking from a stage you don't own, and at any moment your ability to stand there could be revoked. To safeguard yourself, write each column with two things in mind:

- Entertaining/informing your audience
- Giving that audience a call to action that drives them back to your website/blog to access a free value item (an assessment, a quiz, a download, etc.)

Your goal anytime you access an audience via earned media is to convert as many of those people as possible into personal followers. Encourage them to follow you out the door of Inc.com's auditorium to your own. With each year that you do this, you will grow your audience significantly and give yourself huge personal leverage. Without that last step of converting the audience, you're leaving the value of all that hard work with the media outlet that hosted you. Put audience conversion at the top of your goal list when contributing or appearing as a guest.

SUBSCRIBERS

Every time you do an interview with a media outlet, whether it is on a radio station or a blog, that outlet has essentially invited you onto its platform and allowed you to reach its audience. Those who have the audience have the leverage, and you have to work hard to get permission to join them on their platform either via earned media (interviews) or paid media (advertising), which falls into the rented category.

Those individuals, businesses, and other entities that aren't building their own direct audiences as micromedia outlets force themselves to either advertise or hope to get permission from those who have built an audience via savvy PR efforts. This is expensive, time-consuming, and increasingly hard to do as the media environment changes. Those who continue to rely on these tactics put themselves in a very precarious position moving forward.

You must build your own subscriber base. This doesn't necessarily mean charging people to subscribe (in fact, it probably doesn't), but it does mean setting up a call to action on your owned real estate that gives people a clear reason to join your subscriber base.

Each time you give a speech, do an interview, or reach an audience, your focus should be not only to entertain and inform, but to give the audience a clear reason to convert to your subscriber base. If you are a speaker, you should have a free workbook or other download on your website that extends the audience's interaction with your message and gives them a reason to join your list. If you have started a podcast, you need to have a call to action as part of any interview or speaking engagement that gives people a clear reason to subscribe.

The bottom line: When you are on someone else's platform, give their audience a clear reason to head across the street and join your subscriber base. Without that call to action, you will see a temporary spike in interest or audience from that exposure, but very little long-term value. Attention is fleeting but subscriptions give you leverage.

We don't want you relying too much on any one form of media, but it is important to be very good at each. Chapter 4 will expand on this point, explaining how to integrate earned, rented, and owned media channels for success.

4 EARNED, RENTED, AND OWNED— BETTER TOGETHER

THERE IS NO LARGER URBAN LEGEND in the PR world than that of the silver bullet—the one media hit that will instantly transform someone from an unknown to a rock star. We hate to bear bad news, but there isn't such a hit and there never was. Highly coveted appearances with interviewers like Stephen Colbert, Charlie Rose, or the queen of all, Oprah Winfrey, often spike sales of a new product, boost books into bestsellers, and even send customers rushing for the advice of a featured guest or guru, but rarely does one appearance, even with these iconic journalists, mean lasting success. Media personalities such as Dr. Phil and Dr. Oz, who became regulars with Ms. Winfrey, were the exceptions. This theory holds in today's landscape, where the excitement and intensity of viral fame described in this book's introduction also tend to be the standard, fleeting, fifteen-minute variety. There might be lingering notoriety, but lasting power is rare.

So, what does work best in the world before us? It is our deepest conviction that, earned, rented, and owned media not only complement one another but are greater than the sum of their parts when thoughtfully integrated. Approaching any of these alone will get attention, but it will not rival the leverage that will come when used in concert. They are inextricably woven together and are vital to anyone looking to getting a message out.

Tony Schwartz, a *New York Times* bestselling author and founder, president, and CEO of The Energy Project, might well be the poster child for leveraging different forms of media to craft a solid and profitable platform. His tale is particularly informative because he did land more than one of those mythical silver media bullets, but in hindsight, he believes it was his diligent approach and exposure across the media landscape that brought him success. During a recent chat he told us, "There is so much competition for people's attention that I honestly believe it takes many impressions to make an impression on a potential buyer. I feel that about every form of publicity and advertising at this stage; there are no quick fixes."

Schwartz's media story paints a picture across our three primary canvases of earned, owned, and rented space. Already a bestselling author for a book he coauthored with Donald Trump (*The Art of the Deal*) in 2003, Schwartz coauthored *The Power of Full Engagement* with sports psychologist Jim Loehr. The book is aimed at busy executives who demand top-level performance from themselves akin to that achieved by celebrated sports stars, while treating their physical bodies terribly, in a manner no athlete would condone. Together, the authors created a boot camp for these time-starved businessmen and -women to teach them the counterintuitive habit, so it seemed, of taking care of themselves in and out of the boardroom. The book was featured in a segment on *Oprah*. Predictably, it then became a national bestseller, a point at which so many others would choose to rest on the success of their achievement.

Schwartz, however, took the longer view. He kept working on these issues of time and energy, started a company, and filled his roster with impressive corporate clients who hired him to help them do more, do it better, and survive the experience. He wrote another book in 2010, *The Way We're Working Isn't Working*, which was well received by the media both in its hardcover edition and in a subsequent publication as a re-titled paperback. Neither brought the sales success of his first title, but they did attract new clients, some of whom were on his wish list. Meanwhile, his media profile grew. Schwartz bylined frequently for the *Huffington Post* and *Harvard Business Review*, writing the publication's most popular blog for three straight years. In 2013, he was invited to contribute a biweekly column to the *New York Times* titled Life@Work. He also became a regular contributor on network television, appearing on CBS TV's *This Morning*. Schwartz created his platform and grew the audience for his work by using a potent combination of strategy and dedication laced with a devoted appetite for the journey.

So, what can you do today to get on the Tony Schwartz path? Consider the playing field before you and devote your resources to all three spaces. Be democratic, in the truest sense, with a dash of customization thrown in. Everybody and every brand should have a platform that suits their particular needs and goals. For instance, someone who relies on speaking and appearances to generate revenue should gather and post material on his or her website—that person's owned real estate—that showcases that work. A nonprofit organization, on the other hand, might need more exposure via a print feature, in the earned space, to raise awareness of its cause.

Regardless of the specific mix of earned, rented, and owned, there are a number of practical pieces to put in place. Let's dig in.

MAKE YOUR MESSAGES AND INFORMATION MATCH

Imagine this: We are sitting at our desks with a carefully cultivated list of reporters in front of us, along with a book we plan to pitch them. If we are lucky enough to catch them live, on the telephone, or even on email (our first words, by the way, are "Have I caught you on deadline?"), the first thing that a reporter will do is search online for the book, the author, the product, or the company we're promoting. It is crucial that said author/book/company/product have a web presence. Better still if the information we come bearing (current protocol demands written pitches of ninety words or less; verbal ones must be even shorter) matches the message they find online. Today's overtaxed reporters haven't the time or energy to dig for the story. The message and its relevance must be clear and easily visible in the digital arena. If we're telling a journalist that an author is an expert on terrorism, while the reporter's online search for a bio (generally conducted *while* we are talking to them) says *nothing* about terrorism or anything remotely related, we have a mission-critical problem. The conversation and the effort to get coverage for our client is over.

This scenario offers a painful but important lesson for those crafting personalities in cyberspace. Tell the world who you are, be compelling and clear about your background and experience, and make sure the messages you showcase in the digital world mirror those you want amplified by the media. Confusion carries a high price tag in this arena, as journalists simply move on when they can't easily discern if something matches their needs. If you aren't sure how to manage your online presence, we're going to talk much more about this in Chapter 6 as we walk you through an online brand audit.

BE DISCOVERABLE

The number of places that you can be discovered has grown in direct proportion to the size of the online world. Currently, about 347 million people have a LinkedIn account, 19 percent of all adults in the United States use Twitter, and Facebook has 1.23 billion monthly users.[1] In addition, you can also launch an entire website of your own to create the owned space that we strongly advocate throughout this book. More and more are favoring this approach, collecting their content on a site that they own and control, rather than limiting their efforts to building lists of fans and followers on rented space like Linked-In, Twitter, or Facebook. To be clear, you need both spaces to be discoverable in the digital world. Collectively, these accounts and domains are a virtual Rolodex for today's over-taxed reporters. Make sure your accounts are in the best possible shape. Update them often; post frequently; be scrupulous about grammar, spelling, and punctuation; and cute as it is to substitute your puppy's face as your avatar, use a recent flattering photo of your own.

DEVELOP COMPELLING COPY

A 2014 study titled "The Growth in Digital Reporting" confirmed what publicists already knew: digital outlets were, and still are, frantically working to fill the gaps in their online coverage and offerings.[2] From niche topics to international news, these tightly staffed, agile organizations have an unlimited amount of space to fill with quality material. The door of opportunity is open wide to anyone with the ability to create timely, newsworthy, and credible content. While we would strongly advise you to steer clear of self-promotional blather, we firmly advocate that you consider offering your material to an outlet that your first audience consumes. Don't be afraid to think outside the box. Video, for instance, is offered far less often than print content, so be bold and create something in a format that might capture the attention of a budget-conscious editor.

While strident self-promotional material will be shunned, that content you create yourself carries with it the enormous benefit of being positive coverage. Rather than being at the mercy of a reviewer, interviewer, or editor, who could possibly spin your comments in a way you didn't intend, contributing material to publications means the information about you will always be correct and will portray you in a positive light. Consider that payment for the time-consuming effort required to produce highly coveted, credible content.

Finally, view contribution as an opportunity not only to be heard by the audience of a single outlet, but to take that audience along with you. Persuade those readers, viewers, and listeners to follow you from the original forum to your own space. Include a compelling call to action to entice them to make the journey. A free chapter, a quiz, a look at photos, or a video is solid bait for converting that one-time consumer into a devout fan.

MAKE MOMENTUM HAPPEN

Part of the process of getting noticed is convincing a media outlet that a story or idea warrants attention. There are no tools more powerful or more readily available to help you make that case than those in the micromedia space. A blog on Forbes.com, a compelling clip on YouTube, a podcast on Blog-TalkRadio, or a review in the online edition of your local newspaper collectively prove your story has merit. And, for the record, almost no coverage is strictly local anymore. That interview you did on an AM talk radio show can likely be heard via online streaming, and the fabulous feature in your hometown newspaper is almost certainly carried in their digital edition. The top fifty newspapers in America all have an online edition that is accessible globally, meaning coverage no longer ends at a country's borders.[3] The impact of this global access to media coverage cannot be overstated.

Prior to the advent of hyperlinks, publicists dutifully collected, copied, and burned to disc the physical evidence of your coverage. These reviews, stories, and interviews were mailed to media that was, shall we politely say, reluctant to seize the importance of your story, preferring instead to wait for evidence that your idea was gathering steam. These packages of clips and coverage were followed by more publicist outreach, urging journalists not to miss the chance to write about you and your message which so many others have obviously found fascinating. Time-consuming? Horribly. Effective? Without question. That this process can now be duplicated via a quick email laden with hyperlinks showcasing your glowing reviews, your intriguing NPR interview, and your visage on *Good Morning America* makes the art of leverage a new, blindingly fast, and instantly effective method of turning *some* coverage into *mass* coverage. We seriously doubt that the word *viral* would have moved from the doctor's office to the popular vernacular and become a verb (along with *Google*) had technology not made the art of spreading the word so seamless.

MOVE FROM BYLINES TO CONTRIBUTORSHIP

Once you have grown confident in your ability to create content for other sources, make writing or producing pieces a regular habit. This may well be the best investment you make in your platform. Writing for others does not, in most cases, mean that you must abandon your own content stream. Contributing blogs to major sites such as Forbes.com, HBR.org, Fortune.com, and dozens of others often does not preclude you from running that same piece on your own website.

However, to get the maximum search engine optimization for your website, we encourage you to create a separate editorial calendar with unique content for your own blog. Having great content in both places doubles the chance that you'll be seen.

Archiving content is an often-overlooked piece of house-keeping that you should commit to. Featuring that archive on your website, along with LinkedIn and other social media platforms that have this feature, can be crucial in being dis-covered by a journalist when a piece you wrote suddenly becomes pertinent to the news cycle. Get the most out of everything you write. Jot down ideas when you have them, of course, but also consider dedicating a chunk of time daily to search for things that interest you. As counterintuitive as it may seem, Barbara finds that her best ideas surface when she succumbs to that mindless fifteen minutes viewing fashion on Pinterest. You might prefer a walk, a catnap, or a cross-word puzzle, but brain breaks are vitally important to keeping creativity alive and well, a concept that has been well documented.

Build a content bank for yourself as soon as you begin the process of creating content. Keep everything you write here, from blogs that ran on your site or elsewhere to ideas you had but never finished. This bank will help you avoid the diffi-culty of starting every writing assignment from scratch. Take a look at those notes you scribbled about something that intrigued you but that you didn't have time to look into. Be scrupulous about noting where and when your pieces ran, but also reread them to see if they might be revised to reflect new information or your own, newly acquired perspective on a cer-tain subject. If you have written a book, save everything that ended up on the cutting room floor. This material can often be worked into a series of bylines, which are invaluable in pro-moting the book. The hunger for content has never been higher, so invest time and effort into your content bank.

LEAD YOUR AUDIENCE HOME

A secondary goal of all the efforts described so far is to capture new readers, clients, customers, or fans and move them from a public domain to your own. Imagine you are speaking at a conference for a professional organization with three thousand people in the audience. At the end of your talk, it would be smart to walk away with more than the warm, fuzzy feeling you got when the laughs came in the right places, those listening did not seem to be fiddling with their cell phones, and questions after the talk were smart and engaging. All are strong indicators that your message worked. But, statistics provide a more sobering picture. A check of several sources indicates that average audience attention for a presentation is around ten minutes.[4]

Given this, introduce the idea that you'd like to stay in touch with your audience early in your presentation. Suggest everyone stream their thoughts on a hashtag you've created where you can later gather their names. Reveal that you have information beyond your talk available on your website. Or, make a special offering for those in attendance—this can be something as straightforward as a piece of downloadable content, an interactive quiz, or something that plays to a business need—maybe a free flash drive inscribed with your logo. Create these calls for action throughout your talk when it feels appropriate, but definitely do not wait until the end to give specific information on how to get, and stay, in touch.

Use every opportunity you have in front of an audience to move at least some of that group from the physical auditorium they are sitting in over to the virtual space you have created for your work. This audience is particularly valuable because they are already invested. They spent their time hearing your ideas, at the very worst because they had to, but at the very best, because they took away something of value from your talk. Give them more. Reward them for their attention with VIP treatment. Nothing should be more highly valued than a fan. You can also challenge yourself. Devise a way to count how many people visit your site, subscribe to your newsletter, take your survey, or download your content after every engagement. Just by paying attention to these conversions, you will incentivize yourself to work harder at stimulating people to connect.

STORIES FROM THE FRONT

How a confidence quiz boosted audience for a bestseller

Katty Kay and Claire Shipman, authors of *The Confidence Code: The Science and Art of Self-Assurance: What Women Should Know,* already had one bestseller (*Womenomics*) when their new book launched. Both women are experienced, well-known journalists with strong, individual brands, and together they have created a highly respected dual platform for their books. Rather than rest on these past achievements, Claire and Katty wanted to raise the bar even higher. The authors worked with research scientists to create a free seven-minute online quiz that would assign participants a look at their own level of confidence. Every time they appeared in the media or before an audience, they mentioned this free feature. In the first year after the book launched, more than 150,000 people had taken the quiz and tens of thousands joined the pair's email list. In this case, a clear call to action mentioned widely by traditional media created a new and ongoing groundswell of attention, helping make *The Confidence Code* a bestseller that hit the list and stuck.

Teaching kids to take the stairs

In 2012 popular speaker Rory Vaden wrote his first book, *Take the Stairs: 7 Steps to Achieving True Success,* a compelling self-help book that examined our human tendency to take the easy way out. The message was fairly simple: Those who succeed aren't simply lucky or hardworking or more intelligent than the rest of us. Rather, they habitually choose to take the more difficult route when faced with a simple choice. Escalator or stairs? Vaden purports that the mindset of choosing the more difficult method of getting to the top floor serves as training to put forth just a bit more effort in everything you do. Not just once, but every day.

Rory had done more than write a book; he had stuffed his mission between two covers and took to the road in a tricked-out luxury bus to tour the country spreading the word. A book tour is not a new concept, but Rory had a clever twist and a strong team of organizers on his staff. He arranged a series of talks across the country at local high schools, delivering his high-energy message to students and parents. Proceeds from the book sales at each event were donated to the host school to be used for improvements. Along the way, Rory blogged about the people he met, the sights he saw, and the inevitably absurd stories that happen when one lives with a crew of staffers in a bus for more than a month.

These events not only meshed perfectly with Rory's values but also made for a great story, with a local angle and great visuals. Newspapers, radio, and television in each city grabbed the chance to interview the charismatic author, take pictures of the bus emblazoned with the book jacket, and highlight positive activities at a local school.

By using every tool he could get his hands on, both traditional and micromedia ones, Rory created a powerful brand. Today, he has authored a successful second book, *Procrastinate on Purpose,* and hosts a weekly podcast, which regularly ranks as one of the top 100 in the country.

5 DISCOVERABILITY AND THE FUTURE OF MARKETING

CNBC'S HEADQUARTERS ARE AS BIG and impressive as you might imagine.

From the huge satellite dishes out front to the intense security in the lobby, we were excited to see behind the veil of one of the most popular networks in the country and one of the most sought-after earned media opportunities in the PR world.

We had agreed to make the trip out from Manhattan to New Jersey to see our friend Gloria McDonough-Taub who then ran CNBC.com's "Bullish on Books" section, a blog highlighting business titles and authors. She was a very important person to anyone with a business book to promote, as she was the gatekeeper for all content that appeared on that section of the CNBC website. If she didn't see it, read it, and like it, you were out of luck.

We strolled by her desk and it was clear she had a lot of suitors for her valuable feature. There were stacks of books that had been mailed to her from around the country. Although CNBC exclusively covers business topics, it was clear the publicists targeting her wanted to expand her horizons. She held up cookbooks, health titles, popular fiction— even romance novels and young adult books.

Then she pointed us to her computer screen and its over-flowing email box, bursting with pitches from PR reps eager for her attention.

By the time we sat down in the food court to chat, Gloria had made it clear how overwhelmed she was with the amount of information coming her way.

We asked her, "How many email pitches do you get from publicists and others in a normal day?"

She replied, "More than a thousand, and that's not count-ing books that are mailed to me or the phone pitches."

"How do you read through all of those?"

"I don't. Sometimes I scan through looking for an email address I recognize from a publicist I have worked with before. On a good day, I might also scan through the subject lines looking for something that jumps out at me. Often I end up bulk-deleting most of them."

You can imagine how hard this was to hear. Good publi-cists agonize over every word of the pitches they send out, from a personalized opening to a clear reason why the idea they are promoting is a fit for CNBC.

The problem is that in the PR world, there are far more people who don't take the time to send a targeted, appropriate pitch. Instead, they write one pitch and blast it to a list of hun-dreds (if not thousands) of media members hoping (praying) that they will hear back from someone.

The media has to deal with both—and, as a result, every-one suffers.

A series of deep layoffs across major media outlets com-bined with an explosion in the number of people competing for media attention has left the remaining journalists, them-selves a thinning rank who bear the burden of creating more content than ever, completely overwhelmed.

As we mentioned earlier, according to Forrester Research, between the years 2000 and 2008, one in four media jobs disappeared. As startling as that statistic is, when you consider that the time period surveyed is *before* the great recession really got underway, you can start to appreciate why media members are so overloaded with potential stories to cover. The figure below illustrates the decline in newspaper jobs between 2000 and 2012. And that's just one medium.

As a result of all of these things, from the layoffs to the demand for more content to fill the new, expansive editorial space, the traditional process most PR pros cling to just doesn't work anymore. We cringe when we see the amount of money spent on approaches that are no longer effective. Anyone who puts all of their eggs in the earned media basket is setting themselves up for failure.

This doesn't mean that you can't get traditional media coverage or that it isn't valuable. In fact, as we have said, we believe traditional or legacy media coverage is more valuable than ever.

Full-Time Professional News Jobs at Newspapers

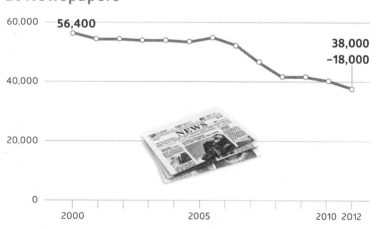

Source: American Society of News Editors, Pew Research Center.

Given this, you have to be aware that the media has completely changed the way it finds, vets, and books experts.

Today, the media is so deluged with pitches that often the best way to reach them is not by calling but by giving them a reason to call you. As counterintuitive as that sounds, media members are increasingly taking a "Don't call us—we'll call you" approach to selecting those they will cover.

A recent Cision/George Washington University study backs up this trend, finding in a survey of journalists that when researching stories,

- 89 percent look to blogs,
- 65 percent turn to social networking sites, and
- 52 percent use Twitter as a resource.[1]

This shift in the way that media members operate has the potential to play right into your hands if you accept it and widen your net around your topic area to catch those queries.

When journalists hit Google looking for a "cardiologist" or "turnaround expert," those credentialed thought leaders who have developed unique and interesting content surrounding those topics have a much better chance of being discovered by the media. Once found, the likelihood of getting earned media soars.

In today's media environment, Google can be your best assistant publicist.

One of our clients, Sanjay Sanghoee, provides a great example of this phenomenon. Sanjay is a former investment banker from Lazard Frères and Dresdner Bank and worked for several years at a leading multibillion-dollar hedge fund. He was an active blogger and worked hard to build a great reputation as a commentator on the financial markets by contributing to publications like the *Huffington Post* and *Fortune*.

In a piece for the *Huffington Post,* Sanjay explored the pit-falls of activist investing, citing high-profile investor Carl Icahn (whom he dubbed a "corporate raider") as a great exam-ple of activist investing gone wrong. He was provocative, took a clear side in the discussion, and tagged his piece with Icahn's name.

Shortly after the piece was published, we got a call from a producer at CNBC-TV who wanted to book Sanjay for an inter-view to talk more about his perspective on Carl Icahn. That afternoon, after a pre-interview with the producer, Sanjay appeared live on the floor of the New York Stock Exchange doing a career-changing interview on *Closing Bell with Maria Bartiromo.*

While our publicists had been working intently for Sanjay, pitching him for this show and many other national TV spots, they could never have known that a piece referencing Carl Icahn would catch a producer's eye. What our team did know was that Icahn was making headlines and by connecting San-jay's message with such a timely topic, there was a good opportunity to catch a journalist's eye.

So what happened there, exactly? How did that post by an author turn into a second media hit?

Sanjay gave this producer a reason to call him because he was in the right place at the right time. As we see from the Cision/George Washington survey, journalists are increasingly going to Google when they need an expert to speak on a cer-tain topic.

This particular producer told us he read Sanjay's *Huffing-ton Post* article and it piqued his interest. That's a huge step, but it's also just the first one. Although the producer was inter-ested, he still had two things left to do: scrutinize Sanjay's rep-utation and then figure out a way to get in touch with him quickly. Both activities rely on Sanjay's online profile.

We expect that the first thing the producer did was see what came up on a Google search for Sanjay's name. It is often said that your brand is what Google says it is, and when it comes to media members pursuing you for an interview, this adage is absolutely true. Once the media becomes interested in a potential guest or expert, the first step is to see if that expert passes the Google test.

After searching for Sanjay's name, the producer likely scanned the results looking for a reason not to book him. That could be an old YouTube video of an interview that didn't go well. A bad review from a recent customer. A website that doesn't look professional. Although we spend much time and effort creating dynamic press kits to impress the media, the press kit that matters most in the age of micromedia is page 1 of Google.

Sanjay passed the "smell test," which led the producer to the final, often-ignored piece of the process: contacting Sanjay.

We had worked with Sanjay to build out a press room on his website, which is a page devoted solely to the media. Our contact information (if you don't have a publicist, list your own) was listed at the top under the headline, "To request an interview with Sanjay, please contact. . . ." Also featured here was some recent press coverage (which tells media members that someone else has already vetted this expert).

Unfortunately, many experts don't make it this easy on journalists who want to reach them. Most are afraid of an overflow of email or spam, and don't list their contact information on the website, instead opting for a contact form.

The problem with a contact form is it is viewed as unreliable by the media. If I am a journalist on deadline and I need to speak with someone in the next four hours, there is no way I am going to fill out a contact form. Instead, I'm going to call one of the other experts in your field who make it easy on me to reach them.

HOW TO INCREASE THE LIKELIHOOD MEDIA WILL DISCOVER YOU ONLINE

It's not easy to get a call from CNBC, but there are a number of things you can do to increase the chances it will happen.

Push out timely blog posts

Every expert and business should have Google Alerts set on numerous keywords related to their topic area. Each morning, review the stories that are running on that topic area, and consider how you can add to the discussion. Media members are searching for resources and insight on topics, and when you create a blog with your take and tag it correctly, like Sanjay did, you widen your net to attract attention from journalists looking for experts just like you.

Make it easy on the media

As mentioned earlier in this chapter, you must make it easy on the media to reach out to you. If you have a website, make sure you have a press room. If you don't have a website, understand which pages come up in a search on your name. For many experts, this is a bio page on their company or university website. Make sure there is contact information on that page. Again, if you don't make it easy on the media to reach you, they will move on to the next expert.

Don't let your social media infrastructure languish

Few things look worse to media members or readers than a social media extension that hasn't been updated in months. Don't set up a Facebook page or Twitter account unless you intend to engage there and provide consistent, valuable content. If you have social media accounts that you don't update, cancel or close them.

Have an opinion

This should be a given, right?

Surprisingly, no. Many experts we see stay in the middle of the road, which doesn't really drive interest or sharing on either side of a debate. Your odds of getting your content in front of a journalist within social media are boosted dramatically if you are writing provocative pieces that your readers want to share with their networks. People don't engage with those who hold the majority opinion—so be interesting and opinionated in your pieces.

DISCOVERABILITY BEYOND THE MEDIA

Journalists aren't the only ones vetting you online—we all are.

We're vetting you if we're thinking about hiring you or your company. We're vetting you if we're thinking about having dinner at your restaurant. We're vetting you if you're new to our church and we're curious about your background.

And the list goes on.

You must stay on top of what Google says your brand is and ensure that you directly control the first several results on a search for your name.

The next chapter will walk you through a process to ensure you control the first impression others have of you and your brand.

6 ONLINE BRAND AUDIT

GETTING YOUR OWNED MEDIA INFRASTRUCTURE IN SHAPE

RUSTY SAT DOWN TO MEET JEFF for the first time at a coffee shop in Austin, Texas. He was a friend of a friend, and they had been introduced because they were both in the world of PR, and a buddy thought they would hit it off.

Prior to the meeting, Rusty did what he always does: he Googled Jeff and spent five minutes reviewing his website, LinkedIn profile, and Twitter feed, immediately forming a first impression of the person he was about to meet.

Before Jeff ever sat down at the table, Rusty knew about his recent trip to the Cayman Islands. His love of dogs. His political stance. The fact that his website wasn't responsive (it didn't work well on Rusty's phone). He even knew about the client from two years ago who was unhappy with the work Jeff's agency did (and the lack of response from the agency to that complaint).

Rusty, like most business people today, had already formed an opinion about Jeff before he even walked in the door, and that opinion was going to be very hard for Jeff to change.

Have you ever thought about how often people are forming opinions of you based on what they find online?

In today's environment, the first place most people will interact with you and your brand won't be in person—even when you're meeting them in person! It will be online—via your website, social media infrastructure, and yes, page 1 of Google.

Do you know what kind of impression you are making? Do you know what kind of conversions you are driving?

In this chapter, we're going to walk you through the first step in every new client relationship we start: an online brand audit. We're going to do so with an eye toward teaching you how to begin making revisions to position yourself and/or your company for success in today's online-first environment.

An online brand audit has three levels: reviewing owned media channels, rented media channels, and channels owned by others (earned media).

As we have discussed, anything built on real estate you own is something you directly control, including your website (if it is self-hosted) and your blog (which should live on your website).

Channels you indirectly control are rented media channels, including your LinkedIn profile, your Twitter account, your Facebook page, and so on. Although you are renting space on these third party platforms, you have a large degree of control over the impression each makes.

Channels others own that connect back to your online brand might include media interviews, your bio page at a company or university you work for, or a Yelp page for a business.

Each of these three types of information work together to form either a positive or negative first impression, and our goal is to make sure you put your best foot forward.

Let's get started.

Imagine a colleague passing your name along to a reporter at the *New York Times*, telling them you are absolutely the best resource for an article they are working on. That reporter enters your name into Google, and we face the first moment of truth in your online brand audit—can you be found?

Many of you will say, "Sure, I can be found—five of the ten search results on page 1 connect back to me." That's great, but the bigger question is how many of those search results do you own? How many lead back to contact information that allows the media member or potential client to reach you quickly?

If the journalist is on deadline and needs to get in touch with you right now, how easy are you making it on him or her to find you? If your website comes up as the first result, that's awesome news—they just clicked through and are now on your home page. If you are like many experts, businesses, and authors we meet, you likely have a "contact" tab that leads the website visitor to a contact form they can fill out to get in touch with you (no spam, right?). The problem is that *Times* reporter on deadline or the potential customer with an urgent need isn't likely to fill out a contact form. They're on a tight timeline and they need to speak to someone immediately. If you don't make it easy to reach you, you're likely missing out on opportunities, as there are plenty of other experts and businesses who will make it easy.

BRANDING YOUR NAME VERSUS A BUSINESS/BOOK/BLOG NAME

This is one of the most common questions we get early in the branding process: should I build a platform around my book title, blog name, or my actual name?

Although there have been many success stories of people who have built brands around a book title or blog name (Four-Hour Work Week, The Pioneer Woman, Shit My Dad Says, etc.), the best decision for your long-term brand is to build it around your name.

Why?

When you launch a website and begin blogging, podcasting, or otherwise creating content online, you are laying bricks in the foundation of your platform. If you are focusing on laying bricks on real estate you own (your website, your email list, your blog, etc.), you are building value on that piece of real estate that you can continue to supplement over time. Going back to the auditorium analogy that we've used throughout the book, we want you speaking from the same stage (one central website/blog) rather than having a bunch of different websites so that you don't splinter your audience and create more work for yourself. This doesn't mean you can't blog for other platforms, but the key focus here is having one central platform you own where all roads lead.

There are exceptions to this rule, but for the most part, don't build a website on a URL that connects to your book title or a blog on a URL that isn't tied back to your name. If you do, you will likely lay bricks in a foundation for six to twelve months; then, if you lose interest or decide to go in a different direction, that platform stays half-finished, and you have to go start over again. The Internet is littered with decaying and neglected owned and rented media channels from others who have gone down this path.

When you build your brand around your name, you're building your brand on real estate that isn't going to change moving forward. You are also increasing the chances that someone who is searching for you by name will be able to find you on real estate you own. We see many people who launch a website surrounding their book title, blog name, or some other creative URL and then can't be found on a simple search for their name. Don't overthink or complicate this piece of your brand.

This doesn't mean that you shouldn't grab a website address for your book title or use a creative name for your blog—it's just that we want you building long-term value on a

> *If you don't own your name as a URL, stop right now and go buy it for $10 a year. While you're at it, buy firstnamelastname.com (e.g., rustyshelton.com) for each member of your family, including your children. This real estate is valuable now— so imagine how valuable it will be to them in the future.*

brand name that isn't likely to change. If you do purchase other URLs, in some cases they should redirect to your website (for example, a book title), and in other cases it can be just a defensive move to make sure no one else secures a certain URL that is close to your brand.

What if your name is taken?

It is getting harder to grab a FirstNameLastName.com URL, and many of you won't have the option to get your name because it is already taken. If that is the case, consider using a slight variation of your name. For example, when David Scott realized his name was taken, he decided to brand himself as David Meerman Scott, a name, URL, and brand he could fully own without having to compete with anyone else. You'll find that full name listed on all of his book covers, websites, and other extensions of his brand. He made a choice and remained consistent in using it. Follow that solid example.

Again, if your name is unavailable, consider using a middle initial, and if that is also taken, consider going David's route with a full middle name.

If you're an entrepreneur, should you brand your name or your business?

This is a very challenging question for many entrepreneurs, and the decision ultimately comes down to prioritizing. For example, despite advice from mentors and others who warned of the difficulties down the road, both of us started businesses that included our last names, a choice that makes it easier to also brand for our names. To date, we've both focused entirely on branding our business, but we will be returning to personal branding with the publication of this book. The use of our names made this kind of shift possible and runs less chance for confusion.

If you are starting a business, you will likely want to start growing your micromedia audience on real estate associated with the business name and then potentially expand at a later date with more of a focus on your name alone.

SEARCH RESULTS

Now that we have explored the roots of branding for your micromedia outlet, let's get back to the online brand audit. For most who are looking for you, the first impression they will have will be provided by Google (or Bing, Yahoo!, etc.) in the form of search results.

Your goal should be to own at least one of the top five search results for your name or business name. If you haven't yet built a website for yourself, the best you can hope for is for one of your rented channels to show up in the results (your Twitter account, LinkedIn profile, etc.) alongside real estate that others own (likely a bio page on a website for your employer). The problem with not owning that first impression is that it lies in the hands of others, some of whom may not have your best interests at heart.

For example, if you are a university professor looking to do more speaking or a principal with a top consultancy, the top result for a search on your name will likely be your bio page on the university or corporate website. Those websites are built to route traffic toward key conversions of business for the company you work for, not keynotes or interviews for you specifically.

This takes us back to the central question in this chapter: if I am a journalist or potential customer looking for you, can I easily find and contact you? If I can't, you have work to do, likely beginning by building a basic blog or website.

Channels you control: consistency

It is ideal to have all of your online channels with a consistent name. When Rusty began reserving channels, he was able to get FirstNameLastName.com as a URL (RustyShelton.com) and Twitter account, but had to go with RustyRShelton on LinkedIn and Instagram, which isn't ideal. If you can, go with the same name. If not, try to stay as close as possible by adding a middle initial or full name when you are unable to get the actual name.

Another level to consistency is the look and feel of your brand. We have all heard that a picture is worth a thousand words, but in the world of micromedia, it can also be worth thousands of dollars if it positions you in a way that makes others want to pay attention.

You should have the same avatar image across each of your online channels. The avatar image is the small image area typically associated with your headshot or personal picture. Many social or rented media channels also offer the option of a header image, which is the large horizontal image that works as a billboard for your profile. Some people prefer to have an image that is more specific to each particular social media channel here (something more professional for LinkedIn vs. something that shows a bit more personality on Facebook or Twitter). That can work, but make sure you choose an image that reflects the tone and quality of your brand.

In addition to the look and feel of your brand, it is very important to have clarity around who you are and what people can expect when they subscribe to your newsletter, listen to your podcast, or follow you on Twitter.

Many people have incredibly disconnected online brands. Their LinkedIn profile hasn't been updated since they got their new job. Their Twitter account has a three-year-old bio on it.

It is important to remember that it's tough to predict which of your channels will serve as the first introduction to your brand. If your focus is on building a micromedia platform that provides moms with entertaining and informative content on how to best parent twins, then every image and piece of content online needs to reflect that focus. If you have old social media channels that you aren't using anymore that are focused on other initiatives, you should strongly consider taking them down.

THE MOST IMPORTANT AUDIT: YOUR WEBSITE

The final component of the online brand audit is an honest, thorough review of your most important piece of online real estate: your website. There are three areas to focus on as you audit your website: your platform, your calls to action, and your content.

Website audit: technology platform

Most people create a website with only one user experience in mind—people visiting from a desktop computer. In truth, people will be visiting your website from many different devices, with mobile (phones and tablets) increasingly leading the way. As a result, the amount of real estate you have to work with can be as small as 2×4 inches to 3×6 inches (see the figure). How does your site look through that lens?

If it doesn't look good, your website may not be responsive, which means that the look and feel of it changes to fit the dimensions of the size of the device it is viewed on. A quick way to test this is to see how big the website is when you pull it up on your phone. If most of the home page appears and you have to pinch the screen to get it to a viewable size, then you have some work to do to get your website onto a more modern platform.

Check how quickly your website loads. The consensus of experts now is that "load time" on your website (the time it takes for your website to appear after typing the URL and hitting Enter) is 255 milliseconds (the blink of an eye). Most websites don't load that fast, but if your website doesn't load in one to two seconds, you're likely losing out on a lot of potential traffic (and conversions).

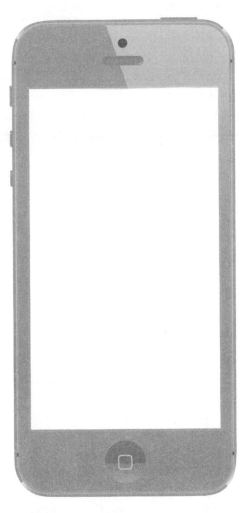

The third thing to consider is the platform your website is built on. There are three reasons we recommend that you consider a platform like Wordpress as the content management system (CMS) for your new website. First, a wealth of Wordpress designers and developers are available, which helps you to keep costs down and gives you flexibility if you need to get additional help in the future or make a big change, like moving to a new provider. Second, a CMS like Wordpress makes it very easy to update and manage your own website without requiring a developer every time a simple revision is necessary. Finally, Wordpress has become so popular that there are many plug-ins—premade programs that add features to the site, available to save you both time and money as you build out your site over time.

Website audit: calls to action

The goal of your website is not just to generate "wows" or "I love the design" comments from your friends and colleagues—the goal is to generate conversions.

What is a conversion?

A conversion is getting a website visitor to do something you want them to do. For a doctor's office, this might be having someone fill out the contact form or calling to schedule an appointment. For a speaker, a top conversion might be having someone email to request a speech, sign up for your email list, or book a media interview.

Too many people spend a lot of time thinking through every inch of their home page, and while that's important, not everyone will enter your website through the home page. In fact, if you have a successful blog, a good chunk of your audience will be entering that way through an individual blog post they saw a friend share on Facebook or Twitter.

Although the home page should have your call to action prominently featured, each page of the site should also feature a sidebar area that lists your calls to action. This way, those calls will be seen no matter which page a visitor encounters first.

For example, if you have a free quiz on your website and your primary goal is to grow your email list by using that quiz, you want to feature it at the top of your sidebar. Below that might be a graphic related to your speaking with a statement that encourages people to visit your speaker's page to download your speaker's kit.

As part of your online brand audit, we encourage you to make a list of the top five things you want someone to do when visiting your website and then carefully review your website (on a desktop and mobile device) to see how intuitive those calls to action are. Are they easy to spot? Is it very clear what you want someone to do? Read your site with that list of five actions close at hand.

Michael Hyatt (www.michaelhyatt.com), author of the *New York Times* bestseller *Platform*, does a great job of driving conversions on his website. When you land there you see his blog with snippets of content and a very big graphic associated with each, inviting you to click and read the post. You also see a very clear, eye-catching call to action to download a free ebook and join his email list. He rotates the topic for the ebook, but the call to action is very prominent. He also has links across the top of his website for people to learn more about working with him, his podcast, and an eye-catching *M* (for *Michael*) that opens to a page of background information. It is clear that his top conversion is joining his email list (from there, he can promote a variety of items, including sharing his excellent content), followed by reading and sharing his blog content, followed by highlighting different ways you can work with him if you are so inclined.

Michael doesn't lead with a sales pitch. In fact, it takes a bit of time to understand how you can hire him. Instead, he begins with value and focuses on creating a connection (getting you to sit down in his auditorium) without any thought of selling. He clearly embraces the notion that if you are entertained and informed by his free content, you're likely to want more in the form of Platform University, his private mastermind group, or even a keynote speech at your next corporate event.

This is media before marketing at its very best.

Website audit: content

We have explored in detail why the most significant part of creating a micromedia platform is the leverage it gives you in owning the connection with your audience. The only way to establish that connection and get the audience to sit down in your auditorium is to provide dynamic content that gives them a reason to come back again and again.

Many people think of content on their website as a virtual brochure, something someone might review once or twice, but in fact, you must go beyond that to create compelling content. Content is crucial to success in today's micromedia environment.

There are three levels to someone's experience on your website.

The first is *informative*. Ninety-five percent of the websites live on this level. It provides the user with details about you, your product or service, and a way to get in touch with you. Imagine searching a website for your doctor and looking for a phone number to schedule an appointment. Or picture yourself scanning a restaurant site for their location. For authors, a website is where you house your bio, information about the book, and links to purchase it. That is all good, solid information, but it does absolutely nothing to entice people to return or subscribe.

The second level is *intriguing*. When someone arrives at your website, can they find quality content and resources that give them value? If so, is that information supplied in a regularly updated blog or podcast? Creating the reasonable expectation that your information will be continually updated and freshened gives your site the capacity to intrigue someone enough to subscribe to your blog or join your email list and take a seat in your auditorium.

The third level is *inspirational.* Is your content so good, your resources so powerful, and the writing so unique that you inspire someone to share your content with their audience? When people share your content, they are, in essence, getting on their own stage and pointing their audience to your auditorium. When this kind of sharing begins, your audience starts to self-propel. At that point, it's off to the races.

When you take a good, honest look at your website, what level of experience are you providing the user?

As a result of reading this book, we want to move you through levels 1 and 2 and climb to level 3. This doesn't mean you have to have a big website. On the contrary, a simple, well-designed website with dynamic content should be your ultimate goal.

7

BLOGS, BYLINES, AND KILLER CONTENT

WHAT YOU CAN LEARN FROM TRADITIONAL MEDIA

ACCORDING TO A RECENT REPORT from IDC Research, 80 percent of us check our smartphones within fifteen minutes of waking up, a fact we pointed to in the book's introduction.[1] That means most of us are rolling over in our first seconds of consciousness to say good morning to our smartphone screen before we even say it to our partner! What did we miss while we were sleeping? Who liked the Facebook picture I posted last night? What were my friends sharing overnight on Instagram? Did anyone text me?

Media and information are everywhere, and billions of us are habitually tuning in throughout the day, beginning with the morning smartphone check. But where did that habit come from? Are you hooked on the crew at MSNBC's *Morning Joe*? Is NPR's *Morning Edition* critical to you feeling informed? Or are you a Reddit junkie end to end, not content until you see the front page of the Internet? No matter your preference, it is content that is pulling us to those outlets during those inevitable lulls when work seems far less appealing than a check of our favorite information sources and tugging at us before we sign off and finally allow ourselves some screen-free time while we sleep.

We can debate the merits of the smartphone life many of us now lead, but the value of having your content available for those seeking it is not up for debate.

It follows, then, that content is one of the most important engines for growing the size of the audience. On owned real estate like your website, your blog is key. In earned media, bylines are fast becoming the most frequent ask from media, requiring you to write and edit material suitable for an array of publications. And in the rented space, writing compelling posts is a clear advantage in distinguishing yourself as well as gathering friends, fans, and followers.

There is no better engine for our platform than a great blog, and we recommend starting there. While some claim that blogs are waning in popularity or effectiveness, in fact, the opposite is true. According to a recent study from Hub-Spot, companies with active blogs generate 55 percent more site visits, 97 percent more links to their websites, and their pages get indexed a whopping 434 percent more often.[2] When it comes to discoverability for you and your brand, almost nothing beats a great blog.

At the same time, it's very easy to have a bad blog, and in our experience, few people approach blogging with the right mindset. It's in this arena where there is much to be learned from traditional or earned media members.

Traditional media thrived for good reasons. It utilized skilled and talented journalists to relate the events of the world in wildly compelling ways. It expanded our view beyond our backyard, entertaining, informing, and exposing us to new sights and sounds. Consider, perhaps, that your own first glimpse of an Egyptian pyramid or a Maasai tribal woman was in the pages of *National Geographic*. Maybe you recall catching a crucial ballgame that was covered only by local radio? Or the television broadcasts that informed you that President Ronald Reagan was shot or that President Bill Clinton dallied with a particularly doe-eyed intern? Newspapers predate all of this with a history that traces back as far as five centuries.

These forms of media were, of course, the only games in town. They wielded tremendous power and were controlled by media conglomerates that created programming or bought up airtime and column inches, pushing individuals out of the equation entirely. But before dismissing their massive power to monopoly, their success should be examined for the techniques they employed to amass powerful reach and exert influence. Remember, too, that before these traditional outlets were faced with competition from the online world, they were in a fierce competition with one another to win readers, viewers, and listeners. Their task was not so very different from what we are engaging in today in this new democratized space where everyone has the potential to be heard.

SIX KEY LESSONS FROM JOURNALISTS

Access to a publishing platform by anyone with an Internet connection and a reasonable amount of tech savvy is not a license to ignore what journalists have long brought to the equation—a talent for finding solid information and reporting it at a time and in a fashion that is understandable and memorable. It takes effort to be sticky.

Know your audience and what they consume

Most people begin this process with an optimistic view that their content, in whatever form they choose to create it, will be equally compelling to "everyone." Instead, give this point a close and analytical look. Do you actually hope to reach small or medium-sized business owners in the city of Indianapolis?

Or tax preparers in Vermont? Even without such a narrow focus, it is very likely that you can put at least some definition around your ideal reader. For those averse to defining the core group too narrowly, think of this in terms of your first audience. Which individuals or groups of them will be most interested in what you have to say? Start here and work backward to figure out which publications are consumed by your target group.

In addition to helping you define your potential audience, these publications can also serve as a guide in determining your authority. Who is a recognized expert in your field and why? Faced with the facts, sit down and rate yourself. Are you trained, degreed, or accredited? Do you have many years of experience? Be very specific about who you are before taking the stage. Established publications can also guide you on style and tone. Are first-person accounts the rule of thumb? Are facts and figures crucial in making your case? What role does opinion play? A close analysis of existing publications and programs are crucial in guiding you as you create your own communications.

New providers should start only when they have a comprehensive view of what is currently available to their target audience and with a specific goal of bringing something new and different to the mix. This knowledge is the first component of content creation.

Create messages that are compelling and timely

Once you have established credibility with your core audience, your goal should be to create content that is compelling and timely. Too many first-timers, fueled by enthusiasm for reaching the masses and optimism about their own, unique viewpoint, venture forth too quickly and risk being ignored. Slow down and look analytically at what you have to say.

Again, these seem like elementary steps, but the massive amount of information that has been pushed into the online space suggests that many feel the new format is license to reinvent the basic rules of good communication. Others who are successful at creating meaningful messages suggest you jot down ideas as they occur to you, conduct a quick Internet search on your subject to assess whether it is new or different, and then commit to a first draft. If you are unable to write a series of simple, declarative statements about your subject followed by at least three supporting sentences, it is unlikely that you have enough content to sustain a piece, whether it is written, video, or audio format.

Submit your work to another set of eyes

Veto power is crucial for new content providers. Working journalists, no matter their medium, are without exception, under the supervision of a group of writers, editors, producers, and publishers who debate both the merits of their information as well as whether it is conveyed in a way that is both informative and entertaining. It is vitally important to develop a process for feedback from peers and experts before approaching the public space. In 2015, a network news broadcaster was suspended from the air for 7 months while he was investigated for embellishing the truth. At issue was whether Brian Williams of NBC News had inflated or exaggerated specific details in stories he reported from Hurricane Katrina in New Orleans and the war in Iraq. We believe this example is particularly instructive because the fallout from those reports were said to have resulted not in further loss of life or danger to those watching and listening, but rather in creating false impressions. Can your content stand up to similar review? If not, start again. There is no substitute for hard fact that can be credited to a verified source.

Involve others in your blogging

As you get started growing your audience, it is very important to involve others in your writing. Every time you interview a leading expert, spotlight a company, profile a blogger in the same space, or review a new book in your topic area, you're giving that person or company a reason to link their audience to your blog, allowing you to bring in like-minded readers. In addition to driving traffic, you also build goodwill and often a relationship with each person or entity that you feature in a positive way. Involving others in your blogging allows you to expand what is, in essence, your own newspaper, from one filled with content based entirely on your opinions, to a more varied publication that includes features and interviews as well. The varied content is more valuable and more interesting to your audience and will make your following grow far more quickly.

One tangible way to do this is to start an interview or spotlight series. Imagine if you had a book that was set to be released in one year, and, in addition to writing timely, compelling posts, you started an interview series and did one interview a week with a leading author or expert in your space. If your new book was on marketing, you could build a list of the top marketing experts, authors, and influencers who were reachable (i.e., not so well-known that they're a long shot), carefully avoiding or leaving off people whom you didn't truly feel had something to offer your audience. From there, you would begin reaching out to them to be part of this new marketing spotlight series. The interviews can typically be conducted over email, so it's not a challenging format for the interviewee. With each new interview that posted on your blog, you would give the interviewee a heads-up that their piece is live, and most are going to share the link on their social media channels and perhaps even in their newsletter, sending their audience into your auditorium. Perhaps even more important, you have also just built a significant amount of goodwill with the people you interviewed, and they are likely to look to reciprocate in some way. When your book comes out a year later, you have fifty-two people who are looking for ways to help you promote it.

One of the things we love about this approach for those who are growing their platform is that it gives you a reason to reach out and build outbound relationships without asking for something. Typically, if you're reaching out to someone with a large platform, you're asking them to endorse a book or go get coffee (if they are a sales prospect), and it's hard to get over the hump because they get asked for things all the time. However, if you flip the approach by giving them access to your stage via your blog, you pull them to you and often into a brand-new relationship that can open doors for your platform and your business.

In addition to formal interviews or Q&As, you can also weave others into more traditional articles that you're writing by quoting them, mentioning their book or company in a way that gives them a spotlight on that topic. When you do that, it's important to make sure they know you have featured them, so try to flag it for them in a tweet or other social media share by tagging their account to pull them in (and generate a share).

Newsjack carefully and respectfully

Competition is a real and valid component when considering the impact of the content that you have so carefully created and produced. Many a good story has suffered the fate of appearing simultaneously with an event or occurrence so disruptive that all other messages are lost. Jack Welch, former chairman of General Electric, was widely considered the foremost business leader of his time. His biography, *Jack: Straight from the Gut,* was considered a major publishing event that met with a then-record advance and resulted in major orchestration of the media surrounding its release, which was scheduled for September 11, 2001. To kick off the launch, Mr. Welch was interviewed live on NBC's *Today* on that fateful morning and was sitting in the green room to record a second interview that was scheduled to air the next day. The rest, of course, is history. Welch was rushed back to his home in Connecticut, while every news organization around the globe pulled its attention and its resources to the terrorist attacks on the World Trade Center in New York's financial district. And Welch was lucky. His media tour resumed in November and his book went on to become a national bestseller. Every other project we were representing at that time was, in essence, lost. After weeks of squirming at the idea of calling journalists during this sensitive time, many in public relations elected to push off projects rather than disturb their media contacts who were now entrenched in the aftermath of the 9/11 story.

On the reverse side, timing your content so that your material or message relates to the unfolding news of the moment can be a crucial component in getting valuable attention. David Meerman Scott calls this "newsjacking" and, done right, it can be a great tool to bring important messages to light. Done poorly, it will be seen as opportunistic and disregarded entirely.

How do you strike the right balance? Know all the details of the story that is dominating headlines and take a close look at how widely the story is being covered. Be sure that your material advances the case, brings up an overlooked component of the story, or is instructive in whatever situation is at hand. We often recommend people consider a scenario in which they would feel comfortable offering physical help to someone in distress. Are they able and available to lend a hand? Are they sure that assistance will definitely boost the person's chances of not being hurt or escaping further injury? This kind of gut instinct to share your knowledge, tempered with a realistic evaluation of whether that assist will be valuable, is the one to follow in a situation where you're uncertain or hesitant about the impact of your information on the outcome. Ask yourself the basic questions that a journalist would: Are you a recognized authority? Do you have a compelling piece of information that is relative to the story dominating headlines? Can you convey your message in a way that makes it relevant to the story at hand? If the answer to any one of these questions is no, hold your content until the timing is more opportune.

Do not rely on frequency over substance

Our collective appetite for information has never been higher. Most of those with the means and interest to secure this book are also likely avid users of the Internet and owners of a smartphone who follow the world in both the digital and physical space. A 2014 study by the American Press Institute shows that 33 percent of all Americans consume news throughout the day across various formats, devices, and technology.[3] One-third of us are tuning in all the time. That represents an enormous amount of attention to be secured, and the directive *seems* clear. The more material you create, the better chance you have of capturing some of that audience. But is more always better?

Participate, participate, participate is a frequently cited mantra for those successful in mastering the social media space, but it is also crucial to maintain integrity of content. More *isn't* better when it is thin, ill crafted, or insignificant. Allot a portion of your time to pulling together a content calendar. It is easy enough to take to the keyboard when inspiration is high, but plan for the times when new content feels illusive. Be flexible enough to allow the timely piece to run when the topic is part of the news conversation, but be certain to stockpile pieces that focus on subjects that resurface frequently or cycle in and out of fashion. A new take on an old subject is more likely to pull readers than a piece that lacks substance or forethought. With planning and work, this content calendar will keep your material well maintained during the inevitable moments when the compelling need to write eludes you.

OUR SUGGESTED BLOG FORMULA

Some who dive in with a new blog know exactly what they want to write about, and if you feel so led, you should follow your gut instinct. For those who don't yet know exactly how they should plan their editorial calendar, we'd like to recommend a blogging strategy that evenly splits your content across three categories of posts.

Category 1 is evergreen posts. These blog posts typically have a long shelf life and aren't tied to a specific time of year or timely news story. This might include posts like "5 Questions Every Leader Should Ask Themselves on Monday Morning" or "7 Reasons Your Marketing Plan Sucks." Posts like these will provide great value to your audience and won't require the back-and-forth of an interview or the time-sensitive hustle needed for a good newsjacking post.

Category 2 is an interview or spotlight series. This is where you can intentionally use your blog as a relationship-building tool and, once a week or so, bring in someone else to share his or her perspective. The great thing about this category is, although it does require some back-and-forth to track down your interviewee, it doesn't require sitting down to write the post from scratch. Instead, write a short introduction to the interview explaining to your audience why this person's perspective is worth their time, followed by an edited transcript of the questions and answers and your post is complete. Interviews give you some rest from the grind of creating so much original material.

Category 3 is newsjacking. As we have explained, journalists are increasingly looking online for experts and new perspectives on timely news stories, and when you connect your message appropriately to a broader story in the news, you raise the likelihood that your post will be found by both readers and journalists. Many bloggers who break into national media do so via a newsjacking blog post that surfaces when a journalist researching a big story online encounters a post on the same subject, generally due to carefully chosen keywords. In some rare cases, those posts have the potential to go viral.

Of these three categories, two can be scheduled well in advance with an editorial calendar (interviews and evergreen posts), which allows you to plan for success. Since you don't and can't know in advance what will be in the news next week, leave space in your editorial calendar to drop in at least one newsjacking post a month.

If you think like a journalist and split your content evenly across these three categories, bring several strategic benefits to your platform. First, regardless of the traffic that comes to your site, you are building intentional relationships with others in your topic area whom you need to get to know. Second, you're widening your net to catch the attention of journalists and new readers who are looking for a smart perspective on hot news items via your newsjacking posts. Finally, you've created a forum to share your perspective on your topic area with your own agenda via the evergreen category, growing your reputation and providing immense value for your readers. If you produce content across these areas, we expect your blog to work as an engine, bringing new audience members to your auditorium with every post.

STORIES FROM THE FRONT

To illustrate the need to bring a skill set to the new democratized space, we decided to check in with an editor at *Forbes*, a business magazine that first appeared in the United States in 1917. Today, it boasts a circulation of nearly a million readers and launched into the online space in 1996. Fred Allen is leadership editor at *Forbes* and one of the people responsible for bringing new contributors and content to the magazine's digital edition, Forbes.com.

Q: **What do you look for when considering someone as a potential contributor?**

FRED: It is a high bar. We set our contributors loose, providing them with an individual log-in and access to the content of our site, so I'm looking for people with clear expertise and bona fide experience who also have something to say and can say it cleanly, clearly, dependably, provocatively, engagingly, and substantially. We must feel confident that they can be their own editor and publisher.

Q: **How can you become your own editor and publisher?**

FRED: Know how to communicate clearly and effectively. It is a craft. Imagine you are at a cocktail party and want to demonstrate your enthusiasm and passion for something. Assume the audience is intelligent and sophisticated, but knows nothing about what you are relating. Practice the skill of relaying the information first verbally and then in written form. People run into trouble when they feel they need to sound impressive or need to rely on buzzwords or jargon. Communicate the way you speak. Clichés lack freshness and specificity. Words like *impact* and *silo* are like Novocain.

Q: Is there a book that would be instructive to potential contributors?

FRED: The most wonderful illustration of writing to inform and entertain is *Politics and the English Language*, an essay by George Orwell.

Q: What is your first instruction to a new contributor to Forbes.com?

FRED: You've got to start by having something that is fresh and interesting and useful to the intended audience.

Q: Can you describe a dream contributor?

FRED: He or she has a strong view of things and a message to convey. Further, they need to have the ability to convey that message concisely and eloquently.

Q: How do you select those who contribute on a regular basis?

FRED: I am always open to new contributors. Despite our robust lineup, I still make approaches to people who would be good voices to add to the mix.

Q: You spent decades of your career editing print magazines. What do you like about the digital arena?

FRED: I love online because of the freedom it gives you. You are not constrained by print deadlines or limited by length. You can change and update material. You can fix the errors. You are not stuck with something forever. I love the interactivity, the fact that people can comment and get a dialogue going. It seems so much more dynamic and vital that way. Right away, you get a sense of the response. I have written things myself that had hundreds of thousands of views, and that's empowering. It is live.

Q: What direction are we going with content?

FRED: There has been a great democratization of the process. More people are capable of getting their messages out. I see an upside to that process. There will be more and more of that. There will always need to be investigative and long-form reporting that requires talent and budget, but new channels will continue to crop up. People have a huge appetite for news and entertainment, and that won't go away. There will be more kinds of media products, but the old ones won't all go away. I don't want to imagine a world without the *New York Times.*

8 THE POWER OF RENTED MEDIA

CAN YOU REMEMBER THE FIRST TIME someone tried to explain Twitter to you?

Both of us distinctly remember rolling our eyes as soon as we heard the stomach-turning lingo ("Tweet me") and swore we would steer clear of what sounded like the most self-centered and narcissistic social media platform yet (which is saying a lot). Honestly, we had enough on our plates—as we're sure you do, too—without having to worry about who to list for #FollowFriday or what planet an @ reply was from.

Putting aside questionable phrases like *tweet, follower,* and *DM*, what bothered us most about Twitter is what we perceived to be a "me-first" focus it seemed to employ. The last thing people needed was another way to keep up with what we were doing.

For example, people didn't need to know that we were attending Book Expo America, SXSW Interactive, or the Writers' League of Texas Conference. Rather, they need to know about how what we are hearing and learning at those places can benefit them. Our tweets these days focus less on lunch and more on sharing knowledge.

Looking back, we were incredibly off base in our initial impressions of the platform: it has become a key—we might venture to say *critical*—part of the work we do with clients in growing large micromedia platforms.

Perhaps the biggest thing that we have learned in watching which people succeed on Twitter and which don't is the reality that me-first content isn't typically what generates strong interest. On the contrary, it is more often a combination of an individual's or brand's own engaging, insightful, and/or funny content combined with a focus on celebrating the accomplishments and insights of others that generates the kind of goodwill that drives audience growth—on Twitter and beyond.

For those who have been avoiding getting more active on social media (what we think of as rented media), this chapter is intended to expose you to the most effective ways to focus your time and energy on rented platforms like Twitter, LinkedIn, Facebook, Pinterest, Instagram, and beyond.

THE UNLIKELY STORY OF CAROL SANFORD

A successful speaker and consultant to international corporations like Colgate, Seventh Generation, and DuPont, Carol Sanford came to us skeptical about how Twitter could improve her platform. In the fall of 2010, she hired us to help launch her first book, *The Responsible Business*. After putting four years of her life into writing that book, Carol wanted to make sure she left no stone unturned when it came to marketing. While she knew the importance of coverage from traditional outlets like *Bloomberg Businessweek*, CNBC-TV, and other major players, as someone who came of age before the massive changes and disruption in the media, Twitter was not on her radar.

During our initial phone call about eight months before her book's release, Carol said, "I'm so excited about getting more active online. I'm ready to make Facebook and blogging a priority." We loved Carol's energy and told her that her blog would be a big part of the social media strategy we developed, but Rusty was clear, saying, "Based on your target market, Facebook won't play a huge role. A smart Twitter strategy will make a much bigger impact with your audience."

This particular component of the introductory call with authors almost always creates the kind of prolonged silence that makes us fear the line has been cut.

"Carol . . . are you still there?"

Carol broke the silence with words we dread: "Twitter? I don't think anyone cares what I ate for lunch."

When we give presentations about the use of Twitter to grow one's platform—relationships with journalists, influencers, other thought leaders, potential customers, and readers— we often look out on a sea of blank stares. We understand their gut reaction. On the surface, Twitter feels superficial, self-centric, and even silly. As you know, we've been there.

Maybe you, too, have heard the wrong kind of buzz about the platform. Most people who either haven't used Twitter or have used it fleetingly (to little or no success) exclude Twitter from their marketing strategy with comments like "Twitter? Really? That's not for me." What usually follows is a litany of reasons why Twitter isn't the right fit:

- My message is too deep for 140 characters.
- My readers are far too sophisticated to tweet.
- Twitter is great for Lady Gaga or the president, but who cares what I have to say?
- Anderson Cooper has millions of followers. There's no way he's going to see my tweet.
- I tried Twitter. No one engages there.

Bear with us if you share these views.

Returning to the noxious "Who cares what I ate for lunch?" line, the answer is often "No one." At least, assuming what you ate for lunch didn't somehow relate to a platform you're building around nutrition or didn't provide a witty response to a delicious recommendation from a top local foodie blog.

Like everything else within social media, context rules the day. As Rusty told Carol that day, Twitter isn't about updates or tweets—it's about relationships.

Within a month of the silence on the phone, Carol had mastered the basics of Twitter, and we had developed a strategy to build relationships with journalists and key influencers in her area of expertise using her new Twitter skills. As a new—and relatively unknown—author, Carol needed to mine every opportunity to connect with influential people, and Twitter offered her that chance.

Almost immediately, Carol connected with Sam Ford (@Sam_Ford), a popular blogger at *Fast Company*. Sam had written a post that Carol loved, and she retweeted his tweet about the post, adding a personalized comment. (By "retweet," we mean that she passed along a tweet he originally sent, essentially quoting him for her audience.) Carol was drawn to Sam's unique approach to blogging, by the way, as he used soap operas to illustrate various business situations. This caught Carol's eye and prompted her to praise his originality. Sam, like many journalists, kept a close eye on his Twitter account and thanked Carol for her comment. From there, the two started a conversation on Twitter about what it truly means to be a responsible business. The connection was made, and when Carol's book was released six months later, the back cover featured Sam's endorsement. He invited her to speak at several business events, and a personal friendship was forged as well.

Were it not for Twitter, Carol and Sam were unlikely to have ever connected.

But Carol's story didn't end there. Based on a continued focus on using rented media (in her case, Twitter) to build relationships with key targets, Carol self-generated coverage in *Inc.* magazine; appeared at a *Fast Company* conference; hosted a conference at Vault, an event space showcasing cutting-edge ideas; and was invited to do some consulting work with Google where we had nailed down a book talk for her.

Crazy, right?

She recalls that her comment when we first brought up the importance of rented media was "I thought all social media was just shallow. Not substantive, at best, and at worst, a place to celebrity watch. Instead, I found some of the most interesting thinkers in the world. And, being an introvert, I am not at all sure I could have connected with them any other way."

The one-two punch of Carol using a targeted online relationship-building strategy and securing a significant amount of earned media put her in position to become among the top thought leaders in the responsible business space.

WHICH CHANNEL(S) SHOULD I FOCUS ON?

There are an endless number of options when it comes to growing your audience using rented media. We often see people either spread themselves too thin by trying to create a presence on every social network they can find or focus all of their efforts on the channel they know best (typically Facebook). Both are huge mistakes because neither is driven by the question you should be asking, which is, *Which channel provides the best intersection between my skills/passion and my audience?* For many speakers, a podcast is the perfect intersection for them, while many consultants prefer the simplicity and familiarity of a blog.

We have seen successful micromedia channels built across every single platform online, so don't feel pressure to follow the crowd down a certain road. The thing all of the success stories have in common is a singular focus on providing valuable content to an audience in a consistent and unique way.

The right channel for you is one where your audience and your interest/skills intersect, and your success often depends on the ability to focus on the right platform. But hey, that's why you're the media executive.

HOW DO YOU KNOW WHERE YOUR AUDIENCE IS?

The demographic statistics that indicate how many people are registered to use a particular social media site is in constant flux, with new numbers emerging year by year. For example, the table shows recent demographics across the top five social media sites.

Based on the statistics in the table along with some broadly understood demographics about the users on each of the social media sites, if you are looking to connect with an older audience, you shouldn't dive in on Instagram as a primary channel. Likewise, if you're looking to reach an educated business audience, LinkedIn is a great way to go.

These aren't earth-shattering insights, but they underscore how important it is to focus your time on the places where your audience currently is rather than where you might like them to be.

RELATIONSHIP BUILDER OR SUSTAINER?

Another important question to ask yourself as it relates to your audience is whether the social media channel you're considering is a relationship sustainer or a relationship builder.

Social media channels can be thought of on a spectrum between relationship sustaining and relationship building. Depending on where you are in terms of the size of your

Social Media Usage by Site	f	y	io	in	o
Percent of online users who use:	71%	18%	17%	22%	21%
Men	66%	17%	15%	24%	8%
Women	76%	18%	20%	19%	33%
White	71%	16%	12%	22%	21%
Black	76%	29%	34%	30%	20%
Hispanic	73%	16%	23%	13%	18%
18–29	84%	31%	37%	15%	27%
30–49	79%	19%	18%	27%	24%
50–64	60%	9%	6%	24%	14%
65+	45%	5%	1%	13%	9%
HS grad or less	71%	17%	16%	12%	17%
Some college	75%	18%	21%	16%	20%
College+	68%	18%	15%	38%	25%
<$30,000/yr	76%	17%	18%	12%	15%
$30–49,000/yr	76%	18%	20%	13%	21%
$50–74,999/yr	68%	15%	15%	22%	21%
$75,000+/yr	69%	19%	16%	38%	27%
Urban	75%	18%	22%	23%	19%
Suburban	69%	19%	18%	26%	23%
Rural	71%	11%	6%	8%	17%

Source: Pew, Fall 2013 Study. Sample base was 1,445 online users. Surveyed major sites only.

How to read: 66% of all men online users use Facebook; 31% of online users 18–29 use Twitter, etc.

audience, you need to make sure to focus your time on the right end of the spectrum.

Facebook, for example, is very much a relationship-sustaining site. It's a great place to be once people know to look for you. On the other hand, it's not a place where people are looking to take chances on experts, brands, or others that they don't know. Simply put, most of us are on Facebook to stay in touch with people or things we already know we like. Thus, Facebook is not the best place for an up-and-coming author or a brand to spend the bulk of its time when starting out.

On the other end of the spectrum is Twitter, which is frequently compared to a cocktail party or networking event, because unlike Facebook—which concentrates on those you *already* know—Twitter generally focuses on who you want to know (or who you want to know you).

LinkedIn used to live right next to Facebook in the relationship-sustaining category, but it has been working to shift its usage to be more toward relationship building, as Twitter is. It now sits somewhere in the middle, thanks to investments in the content platform, the update feed, and groups that allow you to connect with others you don't yet know.

In the next chapter, we will talk in much more detail about how to get the most from each of these platforms. But the most important lesson here is to focus your time and energy on the end of the spectrum that best reflects the size of your audience. If you are just starting to build your platform, you need to invest effort in the relationship-building end of the spectrum. To do that, do at least two of the following things: blog, podcast, Instagram, or Twitter.

While there are certainly some exceptions to this rule, in our experience, they are rare, and following these guidelines will help you ramp up the growth of your audience in a shorter period of time.

WHERE DO YOUR SKILLS AND PASSIONS MATCH UP?

The other important question to consider is what will you enjoy doing? Building an audience is very hard work, and if you don't enjoy producing content in a certain format, it's best to avoid it. If you aren't a natural speaker, leave the podcast behind. If it takes you hours to write a single blog post, perhaps a podcast is a better way to go.

At the same time, it is important not to rule out any platform based on preconceived notions. Many people who end up being very successful on a specific platform initially recoil at the idea of getting more active there (in particular, Twitter).

The most important component of success in the age of micromedia is a passion for your message. As you begin building your audience, you will be speaking to an auditorium that is almost completely empty. You might have a few people in the front row, but you can't count on the gratification and feedback that comes with having a large audience. This is the stage where most people burn out, throw up their hands in disgust, and slink into the mindset that the only way to reach an audience is to buy or earn their way onto someone else's platform.

Not true! This is a case where persistence most definitely pays off.

But to fill the seats in your auditorium, you must give yourself enough time to get people in the door. In the next chapter we're going to look at how you can use a variety of rented media channels to begin doing just that.

9 GETTING THE MOST OUT OF RENTED MEDIA

NOW LET'S TAKE A CHANNEL-BY-CHANNEL LOOK at the top rented media platforms in the world and how you can approach each to get the most out of the time you spend there.

TWITTER: THE WORLD'S BIGGEST COCKTAIL PARTY

If you are a fan of Twitter, you likely evangelize about its benefits to friends and family, urging them to hop on and connect. We do, and one of the hardest things about talking up Twitter is trying to explain it succinctly, in a way that doesn't turn people off.

Many of those getting started on Twitter feel like they're trying to read in a foreign language. It's a confusing experience for beginners, in terms of not only how it works but, more important, the etiquette involved.

Remember, Twitter is frequently compared to a cocktail party or networking event, because unlike Facebook, which concentrates on those you *already* know, Twitter focuses to a large extent on who you *want* to know. If you are new to Twitter, imagine wlaking into a cocktail party with millions of people. The vast room is filled with people from all walks of life, and you immediately feel a mixture of intimidation and excitement.

Just as we do at these events, those in the room congregate in circles around millions of topics—the crowd seems endless, and no subject is off limits. Some discussion circles, such as those focusing on politics, sports, or even the hit television show *House of Cards,* loom so large it's hard to nudge your way in. Other areas seem so niche that only a few committed people enter and maintain the conversation.

Most people in the room have a foot in many of the discussions. They aren't only there to talk about professional topics, like sustainability or small business marketing; many dabble in ten to fifteen different conversations on issues they feel passionate about. These can be as wide ranging as bands they like, conferences they attend, or the game-changing movements they take part in. For example, we have our feet in a number of different circles, including social media, branding, book publishing, PR, Austin happenings, Texas Longhorns, college football, high school soccer, and many others. In fact, Twitter has become one of our preferred resources for accessing news. Rusty actually relies on it more than any other medium. Like us, millions of other people tune in to Twitter to read the latest news, discuss new ideas, find events, and connect with people who have entertaining and informative things to say about a specific subject.

In short, people take to Twitter to make connections and that makes the site especially powerful for thought leaders looking to grow an audience with high-value journalists, influencers, and groups.

Think back to the most recent party you attended, and imagine that instead of going to meet new people and engage them in conversation, you attended to network and make sure everyone knows about your new publishing deal.

You're looking for book buyers. After all, you have a new book coming out soon.

You come prepared, wearing a T-shirt with your book title emblazoned on the front, flyers in your pocket, and business cards linking people to your book's Amazon page.

You walk in the door and see people huddled in circles, talking about a variety of topics. They're going to be so thrilled to hear about your book! In fact, they seem disappointed that you're late to the event because, after all, you're the main attraction.

You walk up to the first circle you see, five people chatting about politics. Perfect! Your book is a political thriller, and these politicos are squarely in your target market. Instead of easing your way into the conversation by listening for a little while before chiming in to the discussion, you lead with the line they've been waiting all night to hear: "Hey, guys, my name is Jake and guess what? [looking around excitedly] My new book is coming out next week!"

You ease back from the table with an expectant grin, looking forward to inking the first order. Not only does no one acknowledge your great offer or even your simple presence in the circle, but they move their conversation across the room.

Yikes! You assume they must be having a bad night and head to the next circle, filled with people gathered around the topic of leadership books. You nudge your way into the conversation, throw some flyers on the table, and inform them that Amazon is running a 15 percent off special until the end of the day.

You receive a similar reaction from this group, although the woman to your left, a few glasses of wine into the night, grabs you by the shoulder and wants to know, "Who sells at a cocktail party?"

You roll your eyes as you brush past her—how rude is she? You've had enough of this party. It's time to take your flyers, business cards, and killer cover design and head over to the family reunion (Facebook), where the in-laws have no choice but to listen to you push your new book.

Twitter isn't about commenting— it's about conversation

As silly as this story sounds, we see this script play out daily on Twitter with people who join the site and see it as simply a promotional tool. Most last a few weeks and leave sulking when no one responds to them.

Can you blame people for running for the hills?

Twitter is an effective platform builder because of the "let's network" culture of the site, and also because many of the most active users are authors, thought leaders, journalists, organizations, politicians, celebrities, athletes, and readers. Together, they provide a perfect environment for brands and thought leaders looking to expand their networks and build relationships with key figures who may just invite you up on their stage, as Sam did with Carol in the story we explored in the last chapter.

Getting started on Twitter can feel like learning a new language, which is one of the reasons we recommend "listening" for a couple of weeks before beginning to tweet on your account.

By "listening," we mean following one hundred to two hundred Twitter users and simply viewing the Twitter stream a few times a day to get a feel for how the site works. It is crucial to do this before starting to contribute content yourself. While it may seem a bit overwhelming to follow a few hundred people, you can efficiently find the *right* people to follow by locating lists from blog posts, suggesting "top follows" in your topic area, and using sites like MuckRack.com. Don't feel pressure to follow everyone at once—it's an organic process, and you'll find yourself adding people as you identify additional media members, influencers, and groups that share your interest or expertise.

Who to follow

Deciding who to follow is one of the most important tasks you have as you get started on Twitter. We see most new users waste time either by not building a strategy on who to follow or by following a few people and waiting for readers to come to them. We recommend a focus on four main groups:

- **Journalists and bloggers.** You should seek out and follow at least a hundred members of the media in your topic area. These media members have the power to ramp up your visibility significantly, and they gather on Twitter because right now it has their devoted and rapt attention. Many journalists are required to have a Twitter account, and even more report using it to find secondary sources for their stories.
- **Authors, influencers, and experts.** Who are the key influencers in your arena? We want you to identify influencers on both a local and national level and create a list within your Twitter account that features at least fifty of them.
- **Businesses, conferences, associations, and other groups.** This category focuses on collections of end users (whether they are readers, potential clients, etc.) and should feature business development targets and groups or conferences that could potentially bring you in for a speaking engagement or buy your book or product for their company. We want you to create a list of at least twenty-five of these.
- **Potential customers.** If your business has a defined group of potential customers, it's a great idea to create a list of those potential clients. This list shouldn't be used to pitch or sell to. Instead, look for common ground on topics and engage these prospects in conversation.

Connect with journalists

As we have discussed, journalists are more overloaded than ever with the volume of inbound pitches from those seeking media coverage, and as counterintuitive as it may sound, Twitter has a lot of their attention right now.

If you are reading this and thinking, "Really? If they have less time, how can they have time for Twitter?" instead consider the journalist's perspective. If, as a journalist or blogger, a portion of your pay scale, bonus structure, or status within your given media outlet was determined by the number of "clicks" your stories received, wouldn't you spend time on a site that drives significant traffic to news stories and builds your personal brand?

In addition to Twitter's appeal to journalists as a traffic generator, it serves an important role in research. Many journalists active on Twitter receive hundreds—if not thousands— of pitches in their email inboxes every week. Can you imagine trying to sort through that many emails to find story ideas? As a result of this overload, some journalists have told us they hit "Delete all" or have a separate, private inbox they give only to personal contacts and the best publicists. While their email inboxes overflow, many of those same journalists might only receive a handful of @ replies on Twitter. Again, as counterintuitive as it may sound, there isn't nearly as much noise on Twitter. For this reason, the site allows brands and thought leaders to avoid the black hole of a journalist's email inbox or voicemail and enables them to connect directly with them in an environment that has their attention.

Before you run to the computer to send @AndersonCooper a tweet, remember: it is never a good idea to *pitch* journalists on Twitter unless they ask you to. The quickest way to turn them off or get blocked is to push a story, idea, or product. Your goal when tweeting with journalists is not to get coverage but to create a relationship by talking as peers on a certain topic. The only way this can work is if you target only journalists who cover your topic area and—instead of pitching or marketing to them—focus on adding to the conversation and encouraging them when you see a well-written article. Use your tweets to offer a credentialed and experienced perspective that will make your content stand out.

Connect with peers, thought leaders, and influencers

In addition to building a list of journalists to connect with on Twitter, make a list of top thought leaders and influencers. As with the journalists you target, you're not honing in on this group of influencers to make an "ask" or push your product or service—you're there to network with them. When you see an author get a great book review or see her tweet about a recent event, find ways to engage with her around that content. Many thought leaders, even very established ones, don't have hundreds of thousands of followers on Twitter, so an @ reply can stand out. Great ways to interact with authors include retweeting their blog posts (with a comment), answering questions they may tweet, and adding insightful commentary to their tweets.

Big data and the power of data mining

In their book *Big Data: A Revolution That Will Transform How We Live, Work and Think*, our clients Viktor Mayer-Schönberger, a professor of Internet governance and regulation at the Oxford Internet Institute at Oxford University, and Kenneth Cukier, the data editor for *The Economist*, talk about the overwhelming power of data in today's world.

The *New York Times* says that the amount of data in today's world is nearly doubling every two years,[1] so big data is going to get even bigger in the years to come, putting those who can harness, analyze, and take action on that data way out in front of everyone else in the age of micromedia.

Anyone who is serious about embracing the micromedia mindset must learn to love big data and commit to consistently analyze the data surrounding their platform. Yes, Google Analytics, the free tracking program that Google provides to all websites, is still the best way to monitor traffic, conversions, and trends on your own website, but that's just one piece of the data picture. Sure, we want you to track what people are doing on your website, but when it comes to platform growth, the more impactful insights often come from data gathered off of your website.

One of the most effective ways to harness big data outside of your website is an approach we call "Twitter data mining," and it's tremendously valuable for content creators who are interested in building meaningful relationships with their readers.

The focus of this data-mining program is to track people who are sharing content via social media, with particular emphasis on high-value targets. For example, when you write a blog post on your blog or a guest post for Inc.com, Forbes.com, or another top online platform, a large number of readers on that site are not just reading the article—they are sharing it to social media. If you visit most of these top online platforms, stories are being shared hundreds and sometimes thousands of times to social media channels.

It's valuable to know how many times it has been shared, but it's much more valuable to know who is doing the sharing.

We don't know about you, but when we share something via our Twitter account, we are doing so because we really like it and want our followers to pay attention. In many ways, by sharing the article, someone is essentially raising their hand and saying, "I'm interested in this."

The challenge for many people is that they have no way to track or monitor those social media shares because the person sharing the tweet doesn't take the time to @ reply them or tag them on Twitter; they're just clicking the "tweet" button on the Inc.com page, and what's hitting their Twitter account is an auto-generated tweet that *Inc.* created. As a result, no alert or notice hits the Twitter account. We consider these to be "ghost shares" for that reason.

However, if you search the title of your blog post on Twitter, it will bring up the tweets for everyone who shared your piece. This can be complicated and confusing if you have a very general blog title because it will pull in tweets that include the same phrase but perhaps aren't referencing your blog post. Combat this by making your headlines memorable. By and large, we find that most blog titles are unique enough that this search stream pulls an accurate list of shares.

Keep in mind that a good Inc.com piece is probably pulling in five hundred to one thousand Twitter shares, so you have a long stream of results to pore through, though Twitter does filter top results to bring the leading accounts to your attention first.

What should you do now?

Each of the people who have shared your post have indicated a level of interest in your message, and we want you to take the next step and see if there's a higher value connection or relationship you can build. First, sort the results into categories that focus on high-value relationship targets. Most of our data-mining reports target the following categories:

- Media members (they can be pursued for coverage)
- Speaking targets (this list can be used to generate speaking opportunities)
- High-value influencers (this list can be used to create relationships and drive new opportunities)
- Business development targets

We have built a program to make this kind of sorting quicker, but it can also be done manually.

Once you have sorted results into categories, devise a fitting follow-up plan for each. Keep in mind that when these people shared your Inc.com piece, they did so without the intention of building a relationship with you—they were just sharing something they thought was valuable. As a result, they probably won't respond well to a sales pitch or over-the-top self-introduction.

Instead, let's stay consistent with one important theme of our method, which is building intentionally, mutually beneficial relationships with readers and influencers alike.

Of the results categories listed here, some will be appropriate to put into a "light touch" pile where you'll simply follow them on Twitter, favorite their tweet, and perhaps offer a thank-you or two in response. The media members list is one to take a close look at and consider what a logical next step would be based on that journalist's beat or scope. For example, if you have a book or product out or are working with a publicist, you could send this list to them and have them reach out via email and say something along the lines of "Hey, I noticed you shared Bob's recent *Forbes* piece, and I wanted to make sure you get this most recent whitepaper on the topic, in case it's helpful for a future story." That kind of email can often open the door for a media hit or a long-term media relationship.

The speaking targets and business development lists require quite a bit of personalization. The best way to turn a tweet into a relationship that could lead to business is by leading with generosity, and the best way to do this is often to take the conversation off Twitter. To do so, click the link in their bio and head to their website (if they have one) and look for a contact email address. Those without websites may have an email address on their LinkedIn profile.

Once you have an email address, send them an email thanking them for sharing your piece. If you have a book, we encourage authors to tell business development or speaking targets that, as a thank-you, you'd like to send them a signed copy for their library. These offers are generally very well received. After all, who doesn't like a personal thank-you and a free book? This will cost you a little bit of money, but few things are better than having a qualified lead reading your book. If you don't have a book, consider another valuable piece of content that you could send them for free—perhaps a whitepaper, workbook, or link to your latest podcast.

The important thing here isn't to learn exactly how to follow up with these leads, since that's really dependent on your focus. Instead, the lesson is to take advantage of the access you have to data like this because it will drastically speed up the growth of your platform, new relationships, and the number of conversions you drive simply by paying attention to those who are raising their digital hand and saying, "I'm interested in this."

Another important consideration in this strategy is to make sure your communication with those on the lists doesn't feel formulaic or sales-y. Follow-up notes should stay true to the etiquette of Twitter. Wherever possible, look for something you have in common that demonstrates you're genuinely interested in the relationship, not just the upside of a potential speaking engagement or PR opportunity. You could mention a recent blog post or reference a joint connection on LinkedIn as another reason, in addition to the tweet, for your outreach.

If you handle your communications with the lists you are building the right way, this data-mining approach will become an extremely important tool to drive targeted results from your rented media efforts.

Our suggested Twitter formula

Once you have listened to the conversation on Twitter, prepared to data-mine your blog posts, and strategically followed people who can really make a difference to your platform, it's time to build your Twitter formula. You don't need to mimic this formula precisely, but it is a good guide as you get started:

- 25 percent of your tweets should be focused on the list of journalists and bloggers. These tweets should include retweeting stories (with commentary), @ replying journalists (tweeting with their user name) in response to their questions or articles, and linking your followers to great stories (again, always including the Twitter user name of the journalist who wrote the piece). The key to these tweets is that they should be relevant not only to the journalist you are connected with or want to be connected with on Twitter, but also to your followers, the number of which will grow as you establish yourself.

- 25 percent of your tweets should focus on the list of authors, experts, and influencers. These tweets should take the same approach we recommend with journalists, approaching them as colleagues and looking to engage surrounding shared interests.

- 25 percent of your tweets should be stand-alone tweets that link followers to key stories, videos, statistics, and other content you believe they will be interested in. These tweets should include the user name of the content generator (author of a post, creator of the video, etc.) whenever possible, but these tweets will go beyond the lists you have created.

- 20 percent of your tweets should focus on interacting with your audience and others who are interested in or chatting about your area of expertise. These tweets will be @ mentions (referring to a tweet including the user name of another Twitter user) and responding to tweets, news, and thank-yous, as well as recommendations of people.

- 5 percent of your tweets should focus on you. That means one in twenty tweets can link to your blog posts, promotions, and so on. While self-focused tweets will only be a small portion of your content stream on Twitter, they will actually be more influential because of the goodwill and relationships you have built with the other 95 percent of your content. Guy Kawasaki calls these tweets part of the "NPR model," in honor of the NPR style of providing great content year-round, peppered with only rare fund drives. As a result of getting quality content most of the time, listeners put up with and even respond favorably to these pleas for financial support.

This formula is meant to be a guide, not a rigid content strategy. One way to keep your tweets lively is to include topics beyond your platform that interest you. Are you a foodie? An avid lover of bulldogs? A diehard Longhorn fan? Twitter works because it's fun for people—they are able to keep track of their favorite sports teams, celebrities, causes, bands, and so forth, along with their business interests. Because of this, it is a good idea to follow people and organizations you are truly interested in as well as those whose business goals match yours. If it's not fun, it won't keep your attention, and, based on what we know about the power of Twitter, we want it to keep your attention for a long time.

PERISCOPE

It's impossible to talk about the growing power of Twitter without also talking about the channel's newest app, Periscope.

As if you need more evidence of how quickly new platforms can appear, Periscope didn't even exist when we began writing this book. Periscope, like Meerkat, which launched before it, allows users to broadcast live video from their smartphone, providing a wealth of new possibilities for those who want to grow their connection with an audience.

Powered by Twitter itself, Periscope allows you to leverage your existing Twitter audience as an initial base for your videos, which can range from taking your audience on a tour of

DKR-Texas Memorial Stadium in Austin, to live-streaming a company meeting, to hosting your own daily Periscope show about the topic of your choice.

The potential for businesses, speakers, and consultants with Periscope is huge. You can choose between public (everyone's welcome—even those who don't follow you) or private (broadcast only to a select group of users) broadcasts and, for those who don't have the time, energy, or passion to sit down and write a blog post, it allows you to reach a very large audience with a more visual connection.

Periscope has massive implications for legacy media and live events, with a particular emphasis on live events broadcast on television, like sporting events. These events now have thousands of camera operators sitting in the stands, able to broadcast their unique POV to their followers outside of the pricey broadcast rights that have been sold to CBS, ESPN, or any other TV network. A prime example of the power of Periscope comes from 2015's epic Floyd Mayweather versus Manny Pacquiao fight. Controversy and complaints erupted when people who paid $79.95 to order the pay-per-view event proceeded to host their own live broadcast from their phone to Twitter followers, who could then simply watch the fight for free via a Periscope (or Meerkat) feed. The fight still scored a record purse, but one has to wonder about how live-streaming apps like Periscope or Meerkat will impact future pay-per-view buys. Event organizers are already responding. The 2015 U.S. Open golf tournament banned Periscope and Meerkat (all live video) and told spectators if they were caught broadcasting, they would be kicked out of the tournament.

We will continue to see live sporting events do their best to control apps like Periscope and Meerkat, but they're likely fighting a losing battle. These two examples are just the beginning of massive disruption that we're going to see from live video apps. The good news for you is that they also offer huge opportunity for your platform.

GAINING INFLUENCE ON LINKEDIN

Against the backdrop of brand-new social media channels like Periscope and Meerkat are social media platforms that have been around for many years and are remaining relevant.

One channel doing a very good job of expanding its utility in the age of micromedia is LinkedIn, which has come a long way from its roots as a business-focused version of Facebook. In recent years it has shifted from being a place where we can find digital résumés, and Twitter-like updates from connections; to showcasing long-form content that rivals what we'd find on top business sites like Inc.com, FastCompany.com, and others. It has also added a feature giving users the ability to participate in powerful, connection-driving groups.

Building an audience on LinkedIn

For years, the only way to build an audience on LinkedIn was to "connect" with colleagues. You could do so either by inviting someone to connect with you or by receiving an invitation to connect from someone who sought you out. With those somewhat limited ways to link together, it lived in the "relationship-sustaining" category with Facebook until its content marketing expansion in recent years.

LinkedIn saw that much of its audience was leaving the site to read blogs and articles on top business websites and decided it wanted to keep those clicks within its own real estate. It launched the LinkedIn Influencer program in 2012 by naming three hundred of the world's top business minds as official "Influencers" on the site. (It has since added another two hundred influencers to that highly coveted list.) This was the first time that LinkedIn allowed users to "follow" updates from others they weren't connected to with the goal of encouraging LinkedIn users to stay on the website to read high-quality business content. The program was successful, and in 2014, LinkedIn announced that it would allow all users to begin posting on the site. With this announcement came a big opportunity for users like you, who now have the ability to grow a large audience here. This is done through the "follow" feature, which lets users follow updates and posts from anyone who interests them. People who "follow" you get your updates, giving you prominent visibility with them. This not only gives you extra eyeballs for the content on your LinkedIn profile, but also a group of people that you can then move over to your website/blog to grow your email list.

The best way to grow your follower count is to share entertaining and informative content within LinkedIn via the long-form posting feature. The better your content, the more it will be shared, giving you access to even more followers. As with Twitter and other rented media platforms, we don't want you to be content just leaving these followers on the rented real estate of your LinkedIn account. Your focus should remain as it does in all rented space: on converting that audience to your email list via the right kind of call to action.

Making the most of your LinkedIn profile

Although growing followers on LinkedIn is important, your profile is still a vital hub for your brand. If you don't have a website or blog, odds are your LinkedIn profile is the most visible piece of real estate that surfaces in a Google search for your name. Unfortunately, much of the professional world still thinks of their LinkedIn profile as something to update and freshen when they're looking for a job and something to let decay when they're not. Instead, it should reflect the most current information about your interests, your business, or your services.

As you set up your profile, we want you thinking visually for the best possible impression. LinkedIn has two primary images as part of your profile:

- **Avatar image.** This should be a high-quality professional photo that is consistent with the avatar you use on Twitter and other social media channels. This image will show up next to all of the content you post to the site and will be what users see in a search stream on your name.
- **Background image.** Similar to Twitter and Facebook, LinkedIn now gives you the ability to have a large horizontal image that sets the full tone for your page.

In addition to these two primary image options, LinkedIn also allows for several different kinds of media to be posted as part of your summary and experience sections. These options can give your account variety and help you make a great visual impression. Media types currently allowed by LinkedIn include the following:

- **Documents.** Although this won't add a visual component to your profile, you can post examples of your work and other documents that support the quality of work you provide.
- **Photos.** You can also post a variety of photos to your summary section. If you are a professional speaker, this is a great place to post pictures from high-profile events where you spoke. If you're a high-quality dog trainer, this would be a great place to post images of you at work.
- **Links.** The links feature allows you to share links to important accomplishments, media hits, and even key conversions on your website (assessment, newsletter, etc.).

- **Video.** We have talked about how important video is, and it's a vital part of a great LinkedIn profile.
- **Presentations.** This is a great place to share slide decks that support the work you're doing.

We encourage you to build out the most complete, attractive profile possible, as it could very well be the first impression someone gets of your brand.

Content strategy for LinkedIn

As you noticed from the start of this chapter, we're very bullish on Twitter as a way to grow your platform and build intentional relationships, but we're also increasingly excited about LinkedIn's potential.

There are two components to having a great LinkedIn presence: a fantastic "static" profile and a consistent stream of quality content (short-form updates and long-form posts) posting to that profile. We just finished talking about how to create a great profile, and the good news is that once you create it, it doesn't require constant care and feeding, although don't let it languish for months or attend to it only when you are changing positions or looking for a new job, as we mentioned earlier.

What does require frequent attention on LinkedIn is both the ongoing content (short-form and long-form) and responding to invitations to connect. We don't recommend that you accept connections from people you don't know, as that gives them the ability to reach through you to make contact with connections of yours. Those people should be following you because they are interested in your content, but don't require that you accept an invitation to connect. We *do* want you connecting with true friends, colleagues, and other professional acquaintances. A nonresponse to an invitation from someone in those groups can be viewed as a personal or professional slight.

As you think about your content for LinkedIn, much of what works for the short-form updates here is what works on Twitter—links to articles, pictures, insightful or amusing quotes, and the like. This will save you time and effort as much of the content you are creating for Twitter can be repurposed onto LinkedIn.

Likewise, the content you create for your blog can be reposted to LinkedIn as long-form posts, giving you double exposure for your single effort and preventing you from having to spend additional time writing just for LinkedIn, something we doubt you'll be disappointed about.

If you repurpose effectively on both short-form and long-form content, you'll have a solid, if not spectacular LinkedIn presence without adding much work to your weekly calendar.

THE FAMILY REUNION OF FACEBOOK

Much has been written about the impending demise of Facebook over the past few years, but in truth it remains one of the world's most popular social networks and is hands-down the most popular in the United States and Europe.

As such, it deserves serious consideration as a key rented media outpost for your micromedia platform.

Facebook is often called "the family reunion of social networks" because of the site's etiquette. As mentioned earlier in the book, most of us are not on Facebook to meet new people or to take a chance on a new band, author, or company—we're there to interact with people, places, companies, and brands that we already know and like. As such, Facebook is not a great place for people who are just beginning to build their platform to spend the majority of their time. Facebook *is* a great place to be once people know to look for you, which is why it works so well for celebrities, popular bands, and beloved brands.

No social media channel can make a piece of content go viral as quickly as Facebook, and whether or not you choose to focus your time on building a popular fan page there, the site can play a big role in your content finding a much larger audience simply based on your readers' ability to share via their own personal profiles.

Your presence on Facebook

You can get active on Facebook in a number of ways (events, groups, etc.), but the two primary routes are via a Facebook profile and a Facebook professional page. Given the statistics, it's very likely that you already have a Facebook profile, which allows you to build out a base of friends and interact with their updates. You must have a base profile to participate in any way on Facebook, so if you aren't currently participating here, a profile is the way to begin.

The second primary kind of presence on Facebook is building out a professional page that Facebook users can "like." Those who like your page are opting in to receive updates and information from that page in their Facebook newsfeed moving forward. Prior to recent algorithm changes, Facebook made it very easy for brands to build up a large number of "likes" on the site, amassing huge communities of fans who interacted with pictures, updates, and other content on a daily basis.

However, as a reminder that *your* page on Facebook is truly rented media, Facebook changed its algorithm in 2013 to show fewer updates from professional pages in the newsfeed (the interstate of Facebook) and, in an instant, slashed the value brands got from the pages they had spent years building up.

What not to do on Facebook

We often see thought leaders, companies, and others start a Facebook page and invite all of their friends and colleagues to "like" it. It is human nature to do this, and our friends and family will like it because they want to support us. They grab a seat near your corner of the vast Facebook stage and wait to see what kind of content you send their way. Most of us who like and follow our friend's pages know we can probably expect a steady diet of promotional posts, but we're hopeful that you'll take a different route and give us humor, counterintuitive commentary, and great pictures. Mostly, we get what we expect, and as a result, you give us nothing of value to share with our networks. We're not leaving—we love you, but we hate your content. As a result, your Facebook page stays at a steady level of eighty-nine likes and you wonder why no one engages on the site.

The problem isn't your friends or your fans—it's a combination of your content and the etiquette of the site. We're not going to share anything on Facebook that we don't really, really like (okay, most of us won't). Even if we do share your content, it's highly unlikely our friends are going to like your page because they don't know who you are yet. Because of this, we don't want you spending a large portion of your allotted micromedia time on Facebook unless you are already very well known.

Parting words on Facebook

If you are an author, thought leader, or business, set up a professional page on Facebook that your fans can access and like if they want to. This page should be linked from your website and blog and should be updated on a consistent basis.

WHY WE HEART INSTAGRAM (AND WHY YOU SHOULD, TOO)

Instagram has become one of our favorite social media channels because it combines what we love most about Facebook (great pictures) with what we love most about Twitter (the ability to connect strategically with those we don't yet know). As the demographic table in Chapter 8 showed us, Instagram's audience skews younger than all other social media channels, making it extremely popular with brands, celebrities, and influencers.

The platform is very simple and almost entirely mobile focused, with a newsfeed (similar to Facebook) that is filled with images and typically brief commentary about those images. Similar to Twitter, hashtags play a huge role in driving visibility on Instagram beyond your base of followers. Hashtag topics range from #Caturday to #TBT (throwback Thursday) to #leadership and beyond, so there is something for everyone.

Instagram provides a bit more behind-the-scenes access to the brand or personality than is available on Twitter or LinkedIn. It has less of a high-end business audience (as a general rule) than those sites, but it is a place where your personality can really shine pleasing your audience and pulling new fans, making it a great fit for many budding micromedia.

RENTED MEDIA WILL CONTINUE TO GROW

As you know, there are almost an infinite amount of different social media channels where you can set up shop, but space prevents us from describing all of them. Some, like Pinterest, are highly visual, while others, like Google+, are much more focused on search engine visibility and email integration. New channels are popping up every day, and by the time this book is released, many more will be available to you.

The key to effectively utilizing rented media is to play to the strengths of your particular platform and ensure that each channel you use has the right crossover between your passion (what you will enjoy) and value, providing a sizeable reach with your target audience. Always remember the importance of not relying too heavily on rented media. You don't want to leave your audience there, you want them following you from the hallways of social media to your own auditorium.

10 WHY TRADITIONAL, EARNED MEDIA STILL PACKS A PUNCH

MARK TWAIN FAMOUSLY QUIPPED that "the reports of his death were greatly exaggerated." The same can be said of traditional media. In fact, we find it almost comical that while a vague suggestion swirls that traditional media is outdated or soon to be extinct, literally everyone who walks through our doors wants coverage there. We've yet to see a wish list that didn't include targets like the *New York Times*, the *Wall Street Journal*, NPR, or another large, national, traditional target.

A long history, a tangible format, huge perceived credibility, and the still-strong circulation, viewership, or listener numbers should be enough to convince even the biggest of social media stars that earned media in the physical world remains vital to commanding an audience. And that is good news, because ignoring media outlets that have been conveying information to the masses for decades results in a strategy that lacks the ability to reach *all* of a target audience. Unless those death reports become reality, traditional media matters.

CONSUMPTION HABITS

Most of the reports of our traditional media consumption habits have largely focused on the declines in recent years. And while some traditional media does continue to lose audience, little has been made of those who *continue* to read, listen, and watch. Twenty-three percent of Americans report that they still read a physical copy of a daily newspaper, 55 percent of people report watching national television news, 48 percent are tuning in to their local stations, and depending on which outlet you examine, as many as 24 percent are watching cable. Yes, the numbers are down across the board, with the biggest hits reported for local news (which we feel is largely being replaced by micromedia), but are we really at the stage where being covered on an outlet that reaches even 23 percent of the population isn't important? How about that 55 percent who are viewing network television?[1]

Scarcity is also creating value—more every day as traditional outlets tumble, merge, or redesign to keep pace with their micromedia counterparts. Conventional business wisdom suggests that the less of something that exists, the more prized it becomes. In a piece in *Newsweek*, longtime technology journalist Kevin Maney writes, "Anything that's really good at getting and holding our attention will become far more sought after—and far more valuable."[2] While Maney uses that argument to support the value of things like the Coachella music festival, face-to-face meetings, and even Costco outlets (which he says demand at least an hour per visit), it is safe to say that the number of those still watching, listening, and reading via physical formats remains a viable one.

In fact, as tangible formats have begun to give way to virtual ones, those who still savor the feel of paper in their hands and still rely on the trusted voices and faces of broadcast journalists will value those outlets even more. Resist the temptation to classify this as a generational divide. As authors who are also parents, we can reliably report that we packed two of our combined six children off to college towing more than seventy books across the country for teenaged readers who have not embraced virtual devices. The jury is out on the four of our children who still live at home. And they are not alone.

In a recent piece from the National Newspaper Network, the message is clear. Naomi S. Baron, an American University linguist said, "In an age where people in their 20s aren't even supposed to remember what it's like to smell books, it's quite astounding that 87 percent of textbooks are still sold as print, even when the e-book is offered for free."[3] The piece makes the case for leisure reading as well, quoting Marlene England, the owner of an independent bookstore, the Curious Iguana. She said, "Millennials frequently comment that they prefer print because it's 'easier to follow' stories."

The rise of micromedia has also given birth to renewed debate about long-form reporting, with many championing the cause, and the expense, of paying journalists to dig deep and cover stories that otherwise might be overlooked. The notion that in-depth analysis typically offered in traditional outlets is a dying art that few are interested in can, and should, also be discarded. In a recent interview, Tom Rosenthal, executive director of the American Press Institute, said, "Research indicates that young people are much more likely than their elders to take a deeper dive into stories that interest them, searching for more information online."[4] What this means is that a story might begin in a traditional format only to gain traction online, illustrating again how the combination of media coverage across outlets is most effective when attempting to capture the public's fickle attention.

Collectively, this information makes a solid case that traditional media should and must remain a part of the effort to gain coverage and credibility. But how can you break through? What do you need to get coverage in media outlets that are operating on slimmer margins and losing audience? Their plight actually offers an opportunity for those willing and able to solve their pain.

CREATE, CREATE, CREATE

If "participate" is the mantra in attracting attention in rented or social media, "create" is the keyword for those who yearn for traditional coverage. Those manning the front lines of traditional news outlets are doubly taxed as they are writing stories and producing broadcasts. As we have said, between 2000 and 2008, one in four media jobs were eliminated. At that same time, outlets were busy creating online versions of their offerings to stay competitive with the virtual outlets that were arriving fast and furious to the scene. The result? Fewer hands to create more material. If you have the ability to create credible content, suitable to the style and readership of the outlet you feel is important to your platform, you are one step ahead of your peers.

From our perspective as those who pitch stories, experts, opinions, and evidence to journalists every day, we see an enormous uptick in the number of invitations to byline. What once was a book review column is now more likely to be a contributed article written by the author. Broadcast outlets have followed suit, archiving audio and video that can be viewed on their websites or even reinvented as podcasts or video highlights further down the line. The time you spend creating content or giving interviews is a sound investment that will continue to pay dividends.

CUSTOMIZE EVERYTHING

As supply gave way to demand in our economy, customization took hold and took off beyond anyone's expectations. From your morning coffee to your computer's home page, we have all succumbed to the guilty pleasure of having it exactly our own way.

What this has done to the art of capturing media and public attention is to banish the idea that sending a generic, one-size-fits-all message to a large number of journalists in the hope, prayer, and misguided wish that at least some of it will stick is gone. What works now is a time-consuming approach that must be embraced as the gold standard: pitch each media person with a message suited to their publication, their beat, and, in a best-case scenario, in the context of other recent stories they have reported.

Knowing who you are pitching—what they write, broadcast, or cover—is the *minimum* requirement when approaching a journalist. As recently as a decade ago, compiling a coherent picture of what a single reporter was responsible for covering could take hours, days, even weeks. Being aware of what *every* journalist on a lengthy list focused on was detailed, heavy work. Search engines erased this issue almost entirely, with the added benefit of the sorting function that allows us to see chronologically what might interest that reporter *today*. Anything less than a pitch that shows good working knowledge of a journalist's needs, preferences, and interests will likely be soundly ignored. An approach with just the right information, on the right day, can significantly boost your chances of getting that dream media hit.

CONSIDER THE CONTEXT

A more subtle component of a solid pitch involves doing more of what editors and producers once did: putting your material in the context of a larger issue. Too often we see great ideas ignored because they are presented in isolation. Rather than asking a journalist to peel himself away from the news of the day or the story of the week, instead approach him with an angle that places your information in the context of a larger issue or trend. This goes beyond newsjacking to encompass a bigger picture. What are the current trends, ideas, or movements within your own industry? Is there something all CEOs are talking about? Is this the year of the woman? Look not just at the day's headlines but the bigger milestones that might be a good anchor for your material.

BECOME A VALUABLE SOURCE

Journalists have always relied on their ability to form relationships and develop sources who will help them meet the incessant demands of creating material. The mighty Rolodex, which now lives in the land of our personal data files, should be viewed as a long-term goal of anyone hoping to grow their own audience. But how do you make your way into that position? Be clear, be compelling, be available when the timing is right, and do not abuse your access. In our experience, those who respect the rules of the road in approaching the media are the most likely to be remembered and, hence, turned to when their expertise is needed. Objectivity is crucial, so before you offer yourself up, first run it past someone else. Just as you probably wouldn't call your unemployed friend to rejoice over your raise, don't approach the media in a manner that smacks of self-promotion. One misstep and your position as a valuable source will be trashed.

STORIES FROM THE FRONT

We checked in with a longtime journalist who now uses her skills to create content for companies and organizations.

Patricia O'Connell is a *New York Times* bestselling writer and was part of the leadership team at Businessweek.com, where she launched and oversaw the Management Channel, the first peer-to-peer thought leadership site. In this role, she elevated the C-suite conversation around the nexus of leadership, strategy, and management. Collectively, she brings more than twenty years of experience as an editor and writer across a wide range of publications, industries, and subject areas. O'Connell is founder of Aerten Consulting, where she helps companies and organizations define their stories, refine their cultures, and create content for distribution across all media.

Q: *Do you think traditional print and broadcast still carry significant weight and why?*

PATRICIA: They still carry significant weight, but less than they used to. The loss is not so much a testament to the quality of nontraditional forms so much as it is to the fact that nontraditional media fit better into people's life- and workstyles.

And frankly, much of the weight still accorded traditional media has a lot to do with legacy and sentiment rather than the fact that they earn and deserve it. Almost everything has been dumbed down, simplified, and has fewer checks and balances with a rigorous editing process.

Q: *The tangible aspect of traditional media, particularly print, still holds a great appeal for a great many. Does it for you?*

PATRICIA: With print, yes. I prefer reading magazines in print, holding them, thumbing through them. But that may be about my own particular quirks. I am a tactile person, so I like the feel of the magazine. Also, I like to read magazines front to back, and I like to skim in a way that you can't do online, even with a PDF or another representation of the print product.

As far as traditional broadcast media, I am just as happy to watch it on my computer. I am actually more engaged with it that way; a traditional TV can be background but a small screen demands your attention. The question is how much attention are you willing to give the small screen, and for how long? We've been conditioned to have our engagement be more sporadic and fleeting.

Q: *Traditional broadcast gets a technology boost by being available on demand via a host of devices, just as traditional newspapers and magazines also get a lift from their online presence. The two appear to complement one another and add value to both formats. Do you agree or disagree, and why?*

PATRICIA: I wouldn't call it a technology boost or a prestige boost but a convenience boost. Although I prefer to read a magazine in print, sometimes it is easier to look at it online, and of course the abilities to search, scale, and share any kind of media online are huge pluses.

The added value is in the ability to be on demand and easily accessible and available.

Q: *Long-form reporting has been the strength of many of our most esteemed traditional media outlets—from the* New York Times *to* The New Yorker, 60 Minutes, *and even NPR. Do you believe there is still a place for it in our fast-paced world?*

PATRICIA: The societal need for serious, in-depth reporting and editing has not changed. The willingness to do them has.

Thomas Jefferson once said (allegedly, because I read it online), "Were it left to me to decide whether we should have a government without newspapers, or newspapers without a government, I should not hesitate a moment to prefer the latter." Of course, he was referring to a time where news was very greatly defined by the parameters around creation and delivery. Those have disappeared. Where does that leave his quote and sentiment now?

Q: *You have edited and written for both traditional and online publications. Do you favor one over another?*

PATRICIA: What I care about is the ability and the freedom to do high-quality work. That doesn't always mean a great deal of reporting; for thought leadership, it is about a well-argued, well-informed position rather than one imbued merely by passion and opinion.

Whether it is reporting or drawing the best out of great thinkers who may not be great writers, it is about a combination of time and money. There is less inclination to give writers and editors enough of either, let alone both, to do high-quality work. As a freelance writer or writer for hire, you can incur a financial hit by taking the time so that it doesn't appear cost-effective for the client.

As an editor, you often can't pay people as much as you'd like to or as they deserve, so one or both of you has to pick up the slack/take the hit. Online, there can be too much pressure to produce content that will merely draw eyeballs and visitors and that is less than substantive and brand-appropriate, which ultimately changes what is brand-appropriate.

Q: *What do delivery methods mean for the traditional forms of content?*

PATRICIA: The first major shift in terms of content quality was the addition of a twenty-four-hour news cycle on TV. It was not when people got their news from TV instead of radio, or from radio instead of newspapers. When we first had a twenty-four-hour TV news cycle, you saw the same story/content/footage being shown over and over, because the ability to create content had not caught up with the ability to deliver it.

The ability to create content, curate it, and share it is now in the hands of anyone and everyone, whether they are "qualified" to do so and whether the appropriate checks and balances are in place. So it's about quality. It's what I keep coming back to, because it is critical.

There used to be constraints in terms of ability to create and deliver content that made quality possible and profitable—and expected. Granted, there were always different standards and levels of quality—a tabloid versus a broadsheet; an in-depth, much-reported story versus breaking news. But outlets knew the league in which they were playing.

The bar has been lowered for everyone, and many outlets seem happy just to graze it. A few places still aim for the heights that they did years ago without thinking about where the bar is— NPR and *The New Yorker*. That's about it, I think.

The real issues about traditional media are in terms of quality of content, and how does it get paid for? Is the answer people like Jeff Bezos and John Henry owning papers that may not be profitable, and perhaps taking them on as altruistic, public service endeavors? Will they use their business acumen to monetize them, or their business success to subsidize them?

11 TAKE THE STAGE

LAUNCH A SPEAKING CAREER

IN 2009, ACTOR ASHTON KUTCHER MADE HEADLINES when he set the lofty goal of collecting a million fans on his Facebook page. Next, he challenged CNN to a race for a million Twitter followers and won. In addition to amassing the audiences, the Twitter race was staged with the express goal of securing a donation of ten thousand mosquito nets for World Malaria Day. CNN lost the bet, bought the nets, and the story got the attention Kutcher was hoping for.[1] In a post on the push for fans, Mashable's Adam Ostrow wrote, "Hopefully, Kutcher and [then] wife Demi Moore will continue to use their massive new platform for good."[2] In 2015, Kutcher used his enormous online following to launch A Plus, a hub for stories that make a difference and create positive societal change, which is among the top fifty popular websites nationwide with thirty million unique monthly viewers.[3]

While few have the ability to attract such a large following, this story does illustrate a crucial but often overlooked component of building thought leadership status and a personal platform: what should you do with the audience you amass? Ideally, that engaged audience is the first step in creating a new and profitable market for your work. For many, this is the primary goal. Whether you hope to pack your suitcase for hundreds of gigs or hanker to secure just ten dates annually to address your core audience, would-be speakers need a specific set of tools and material to break into an area dominated by celebrities, former presidents, and captains of industry who routinely take in six figures for a single appearance.

The speaking business was hit very hard in the wake of 9/11 when business travel and large gatherings were put on hold in the wake of the terrorist attacks. It got another punch in 2008 when the economic downturn brought big slashes to meeting budgets. But it has enjoyed a renaissance in recent years. This restart can serve the novice well. Those just beginning will benefit as the rules are rewritten to accommodate shrinking attention spans, the hunger for entertainment, and the rising value of face-to-face contact with experts. Tailor your talks with those three components in mind, and you'll bring a decided advantage.

IDENTIFY YOUR AUDIENCE

Just as we suggested that you think carefully about the first audience for your media messages, you must consider the target audience for a live presentation. Start with a look at who is following you on social media or has subscribed to your newsletter or blog. Are HR executives drawn to your information about managing several generations in the workplace? Did the piece you wrote about executing change prove to be sticky with the C-suite and management crowd? All of these are clues that will help you move from a wide, ill-defined general audience to a group that is particularly impacted by problems or issues you can address.

Move next to professional organizations that those in your target audience belong to. Add in the professional organizations of which you are a member. Log on to your LinkedIn profile and search for groups related to or impacted by issues that fall within your area of expertise. Join these and consider starting your own group. Attend as many professional gatherings in your area as possible to network with those currently working in the industry.

Finally, start focusing on trending issues in the industries you hope to engage with. Read the trade and professional journals associated with those sectors of business, and become aware of the current conversation and pressing issues. Once briefed, commit to blogging on the subjects where your experience and expertise applies and where you can bring a compelling new voice to the conversation. The content you create in print form can serve as the basis for a presentation when you book your first appearance.

PERFECT YOUR PERFORMANCE SKILLS

If you have watched Tiger Woods hit a golf ball, Michael Phelps swim a lap, or Warren Buffet invest a million, you have likely bought into the conventional wisdom that innate talent trumps all. But British-based researchers Michael J. Howe, Jane W. Davidson, and John A. Sluboda are among those who say otherwise. In an extensive 2006 study, the researchers concluded, "The evidence we have surveyed . . . does not support the [notion that] excelling is a consequence of possessing innate gifts."[4] In a piece in *Fortune* written in the wake of that study, senior editor Geoff Colvin reported, "[T]he striking, liberating news is that greatness isn't reserved for a preordained few. It is available to you and to everyone."[5]

Start with hard work. If your current occupation doesn't require you to share your knowledge before a group, find ways to introduce presentation into your daily routine. Ask for ten minutes at the next meeting you attend to brief everyone on the project you're working on. Challenge yourself to create a slide deck to go along with that blog you just posted or that piece you contributed to Forbes.com. Commit to researching evidence to inform your point of view. Explore visual elements that will reinforce your information.

Once you've put together a presentation, practice it every day. If you cannot bear the thought of stepping in front of a live audience, park yourself in front of your phone's video function and record yourself presenting solo. Watch critically, and do it again. As Malcolm Gladwell suggests in *Outliers,* with ten thousand hours of practice, it is possible to achieve mastery.[6] The majority of us without ten thousand hours to spare can still improve our skills with less time but a steady commitment to rehearsing.

REPRESENT YOUR SKILLS

Too many people stop once they have developed sharp presentation skills, an enviable roster of contacts, and a sizeable following for their content, both online and off. They fail to package this information in a way that specifically sells them as speakers. Without it, you are making a blind assumption that anyone reading your profile on a rented platform like LinkedIn or Twitter or even your website, the space you own and control, will somehow discern that you are available to present. Build the skills to be a successful speaker, and then showcase them in the form of what is called a speaker's kit. Add the title "speaker" on all of your online profiles and even in the byline of contributions you make to publications. Give a clear indication that you are available for speeches and live talks.

Revise your bio so that it includes and highlights your public speaking appearances. Create a list of topics, typically between four and eight, that you can address in a presentation. Include a description of your written work, both white papers and books, along with reviews or praise of those materials. Showcase a list of venues and clients where you have appeared and, if possible, any feedback you got from those engagements. Invest in good-quality video of yourself. Twenty to thirty minutes of your presentation before a live audience is ideal, signaling to potential customers your ability to sustain a message and engage a crowd. Hire a professional to edit the material so that it is bookended at the start with a screen shot of the book's jacket, title of your talk, the venue, and the date of your speech, and at the end, with your social media coordinates. We're repeatedly asked whether a composite or highlight reel with clips from a variety of talks can be used. These clip reels can be compelling if carefully used on your website, but they aren't useful for event planners trying to determine if you can command the stage, deliver information, and entertain and engage the audience over a longer period of time. To be safe, invest in both versions of your performances.

House your speaking kit on your website, and provide clear instructions and contact information for inquiries. Don't send these to an anonymous blind box, but one that you or someone on your staff will check daily. Like the media, many of those hiring speakers will simply move on if they can't make contact with you quickly.

Finally, avoid giving a fee structure on your website, but instead offer to create a customized package for the potential buyer to consider. Set up an introductory phone call to determine specifics of the assignment, number of attendees, focus of the event, and expectations for the talk. With this information, you can decide whether this is an assignment you would relish or merely endure, and set your price accordingly. Be open to taking less compensation for a talk if the engagement will add credibility and cachet to your profile.

DON'T REFUSE UNPAID ENGAGEMENTS

Breaking into any business is generally difficult, and speaking is by no means an exception. Do not focus on securing a TED talk as you embark on a new career, but rather think small and local. Investigate opportunities at Chambers of Commerce, Rotary Clubs, Toastmasters, and any trade organizations that have a local chapter. Attend meetings and networking events, develop a presentation, and then approach with a request to address the group. Practicing before someone other than your mirror or your partner is an excellent start, but taking the stage before a live group is invaluable.

In a piece in *Forbes* magazine, consultant and personal development coach Chris Widener recounts his twenty-five-year journey to become a full-time professional speaker that began by speaking at high schools and summer camps.[7] To grow the size of his audience and move on to paid engagements, he honed his performance skills in those unpaid gigs, while taking to the Internet to create content. "When the Internet opened up," he writes, "everyone had a website, but no one had content. I wrote 450 articles on success and business and gave it away. At the bottom, the articles would give my bio. I was able to build a list of 100,000 followers really quickly." And the speaking gigs followed, allowing Widener to make speaking his primary career.

AMPLIFY YOUR MESSAGE WITH SOCIAL MEDIA

We live in an era where the impact of a live speech doesn't end in the auditorium but extends into the online space. YouTube can hold an archive video of the talk, making it available for view by its billion users.[8] Twitter not only can help us start a conversation among the audience, but can keep it going long after the live event is a memory. Just as writing is an investment that pays big dividends when it comes to remaining in the public eye, so does chatter that persists after your performance.

Make it easy for your audience to coalesce into a community by creating a hashtag for your talk, displaying it onstage from the podium, and periodically urging those in the audience to join that online conversation. Be certain your presentation has a slide with your own social media coordinates and show it during the event and particularly at the end, to encourage those in attendance to stay in touch with any thoughts or questions. Be certain to thank those who do reach out, and invite them to take a look at your website where they might subscribe to your blog or newsletter list. A goal of your live event, besides being entertaining and relevant, should be to grow your email list with those in the room by bringing them over to your website to learn more.

SELL TO THE AUDIENCE—WITH TACT

While the first goal of a speaker is to entertain and inform the audience, it is also a chance to interact directly with potential customers. A Harris Poll concluded that face-to-face contact with customers remains the most effective way to make a sale.[9] Seize the opportunity and expand the impact that a speech can have on your business.

Take a close look at your offerings to determine which products or services produce revenue. Craft a concise paragraph describing those offerings. Ideally, add a list of clients you have worked with and, just as you did when creating your speakers kit, include testimonials. Books are a relatively simple commodity to offer while speaking, as they can be sold at the back of the room or be purchased by the event organizer for everyone in attendance.

Aim for events that will bring together those who hire you most frequently. If you are a consultant advising on customer acquisition, a group of chief marketing officers would be fertile ground for attracting new business. Again, this is an instance where a niche audience is not only important but frequently the most lucrative. Speak with an eye toward gaining new fans, followers, and customers.

JOIN AN ASSOCIATION

There are a handful of groups for public speakers, from Toastmasters International, which was designed to help people develop their speaking skills, to the Global Speaker Federation, which works to unite speakers the world over. The best-known and most recognizable among the existing groups is the National Speakers Association (NSA).

Founded in 1973, the NSA offers a wealth of information for members. Its mission is to provide education and business knowledge to support those in the speaking profession (see NSASpeakers.org). Receiving formal recognition from the NSA, particularly a nomination to the group's Hall of Fame, brings enormous credibility and a competitive advantage in securing paid talks. The NSA also boasts hundreds of local chapters that host meet-ups where speakers can present to an audience of peers. Attend a local meeting and start networking with other speakers. The informal sharing at these meetings may provide just the inspiration and direction you need to either begin or ramp up a speaking career.

ENGAGE A BUREAU

Once you have created the speaker's kit described earlier in this chapter, spent time practicing your presentation skills, and secured a few unpaid talks, the time is likely right to consider representation by an agency. In exchange for a percentage of your fees, speaking bureaus bring working knowledge of price range; access to a database of meeting planners, event organizers, and companies that hire talent for their corporate events; keen negotiation skills; and a practiced eye for reviewing contracts.

Listing with a bureau is a solid method of getting exposure for the speaking part of your platform. The more you become known for speaking, the more likely you are to build this into a solid revenue stream. Before you sign up, understand that you will be competing with your peers as agencies typically list multiple experts in each category. Rather than choosing a group that demands an exclusive agreement, cast your net wide and list with several bureaus to increase your chances of being booked. If you are an author, ask your publishing house if they have an in-house speaking division. Many have created these divisions with a goal of keeping sales going after a book's launch.[10]

Finally, don't rely on representation by a bureau as the sole method of bringing in business. Do the virtual equivalent of hanging out your shingle by creating a button on your website to hold all of your speaking materials complete with an email and phone number so you can respond rapidly and directly to inbound requests.

SPEAK VIRTUALLY

One of the perks of growing your micromedia audience is the ability to attract an audience to virtual presentations, including webinars and teleseminars. Popular webinar technology services like GoToMeeting or GoToWebinar allow you to give a presentation to an audience that can tune in from anywhere with Internet access. Webinars can be a great way to provide value to your audience and to promote services, products, or other offerings. Although there is plenty of prestige in taking a "real" stage at an event, don't discount the opportunities now available to you to reach your audience online via virtual speaking engagements.

STORIES FROM THE FRONT

Jackie Huba is a popular corporate speaker, author of three books on customer loyalty, and consultant to leading companies such as Discovery Communications, Whirlpool, Dell, and Kraft, where she advised on how to create more loyalty in their customer base.

Named as one of the ten most influential online marketers, Jackie is a regular contributor to Forbes.com and for a decade coauthored the award-winning Church of the Customer blog, which boasted more than 105,000 readers. Her work has frequently been featured in the media, such as the *Wall Street Journal,* the *New York Times, Businessweek,* and *Advertising Age.* She was a founding board member of the Word of Mouth Marketing Association.

Q: *You are an accomplished author and speaker. How do the two roles work together?*

JACKIE: When I first started as a marketing consultant, I realized it would be really great to have a tagline, something that encapsulates what you do. "Creating customer evangelists" was the first tagline I used. I also wanted a book to encapsulate my ideas into one place. If you want to stand out, a book becomes a necessary tool. Today, I do 90 percent speaking and 10 percent consulting. 9/11 killed the speaking gig and turned those people into consultants. Right now, we are seeing that trend reverse.

Q: *We have seen you speak, and you are incredibly dynamic. What's your advice for someone getting started?*

JACKIE: People need to think about speaking completely differently. I used to think I had to cover *all* of the main concepts in my book in a single speech. What I have come to realize is that I am a performer first. People want takeaways and big ideas; but they also want engagement, entertainment, and a show. Cut the content down and focus on delivery and relating to your audience. Take an improv or stand-up class. Get comfortable with being live and real with your audience. Be ready to deal with the unexpected. When people think they have to speak, they feel they are the center of attention. TED has helped people think that way. I personally think that when you are in a live event, you want to create an experience that the audience walks away with. It makes people pay attention, not just listen.

Q: *Bureaus versus self-generated gigs—which do you do? Both? More of one than the other?*

JACKIE: This has completely changed in the past ten years. I have two bureaus that make up 80 percent of my speaking engagements. The other 20 percent come via online discoverability or referral. During 2003–2007, most leads were self-generated. It was a lot of work (travel, negotiation, etc.), but having that taken care of costs a commission.

Q: *What kind of audiences do you most prefer to address?*

JACKIE: Super-energetic audiences are best. Skeptical audiences that are overly analytical are not my favorite.

Q: *How do you promote your book without sounding like you are giving an infomercial?*

JACKIE: I show a picture of the book on a slide. I refer to the information that I am about to present as being included in the book, but I make it clear there are many more strategies in the book that I can't get to in the talk because of time constraints.

Q: *What's your favorite call to action at the end of the speech? How do you get people to leave the auditorium and follow you into your own space, or website, as is most likely the case?*

JACKIE: You have to be clear about what you are offering or who you want to be in touch with. Leave your card at the back of the room for attendees so they have a way to be in touch. Put your contact information on the first slide, including your hashtag. Repeat it at the end of the talk. Ask the audience what they heard that interests them, and ask them to tweet it to you. Use that to develop another speech or a workshop that covers the hot button issues.

Q: *What is your favorite thing about what you do?*

JACKIE: I love being on stage, but honestly, the best thing that happens is when someone tells me they have read my book and it completely changed how they looked at their work. If I change one life, I have really done my job.

12 | FUTUREPROOF YOUR MEDIA STRATEGY

BASEBALL GREAT ROGER MARIS ONCE SAID, "You hit home runs not by chance, but by preparation." This advice is particularly relevant as you prepare to step into an unknown media landscape that has reinvented itself in the span of a few decades and that shows every indication of evolving further at increasingly blinding speed. Whether you are drawn to the latest app or digital tool, or become overwhelmed at the prospect of mastering a new method of communication, there is no time like the present to dive in. With preparation, you will be ready for the evolving media landscape.

Predicting the future of media is largely folly. But experts do agree that technology will continue to change the way we live and work, and globalization will become even more deeply entrenched in our society as information flows seamlessly across geographical borders. Longtime journalist Eric Pfanner notes, "The convergence of digital media and technology, underway since the dawn of the Internet, will accelerate. Distinctions between old and new media will fade; and most media will be digital." He further suggests that as new platforms for consumption evolve, media content will become more important.[1] That growing need for content is important, even crucial. Those who create it will remain relevant and visible despite the tsunami of change.

We have sounded the bell repeatedly in this book about the importance of content. With that point made, we'd like to give you more tangible ways to create a platform, work on an existing one, or take the next step to become a micromedia outlet in your own right. What can you do once you have turned yourself into a tight and effective content creator? Will every step on the path to emerging as a thought leader in your own field be this hard? We won't delude you by saying it will all be easy, but the steps described in this chapter should be less time-consuming and not quite as painstaking as writing original, factual, fascinating material. With some hard work, a few lists, and a bit of time to think deep and hard, creating a media presence in an uncertain world is an attainable goal.

SIX WAYS TO FUTUREPROOF YOUR MEDIA PRESENCE

When developing a strategy to stay in public view, we urge you to commit to a long-term plan for breakout success. As tempting as it is to take what you think may be a quick path to visibility by copying the route someone else took or by trying to emulate the most recent incident of something going viral, most people are better served with a solid strategy to create and sustain slow and steady momentum.

Become Discoverable

It is no secret that today's journalist searches for story ideas and sources in the online space. What once was the domain of the intrepid reporter hungry for facts and willing to traverse the world is now accomplished with an exceedingly short trip to the office or laptop, access to global information at the press of a button, and a few well-chosen search words. As mentioned earlier in the book, a 2010 study conducted by Cision (a media database firm) and George Washington University revealed that

89 percent of working journalists look to blogs for story research, 65 percent to social media sites such as Facebook and LinkedIn, and 52 percent to microblogging services such as Twitter.[2] But before you fire your public relations staff, close your meetings to the public, or decide that an Instagram campaign can replace releasing a white paper, please read further with a discerning eye and working knowledge of how *primary* research (facts collected firsthand) for a story differs from *secondary* research (summation of existing research or collection of collaborating evidence). The same survey of more than 9,100 journalists reveals that 84 percent of those reporters said social media was anywhere from "slightly less" to "much less" reliable than traditional, primary sources. In deference to our own profession, 44 percent of them considered PR professionals to be "key" in their *primary research* for stories. All of which is to say, you need both.

Journalist Brenda Ehrlich makes the case that participating in social media can boost your chance of coming to the attention of the media.[3] From finding leads to noticing trends, crowdsourcing to sharing stories, Ehrlich's piece offers abundant examples of how experts, authors, and other thought leaders found fame in the public eye because they were discoverable online. Moreover, these aren't limited to features or fluff pieces. Ehrlich reports:

> Aaron Lazenby, a DJ for Pirate Cat Radio, was scanning Twitter one night last year when he noticed #iranelection trending. Curious, he clicked on the hashtag and started poring over the flood of tweets about the "stolen" election.
>
> Lazenby became fascinated with the situation and stayed up all night talking with people in Iran and reading up on the subject. The next day, he was hanging out with a Pulitzer Prize–winning AP reporter who was completely unaware of what was going on in Iran—news of the protests had not reached the mainstream news. Lazenby seized the opportunity to tell the story.

He contacted one of his Twitter sources, who agreed to do an interview over Skype for Lazenby's radio show. The interview, in turn, was picked up by CNN's iReport, a citizen journalism portal.

"Our interactions on Twitter built enough trust between us where he was comfortable talking to me and I was comfortable using him as a source," Lazenby says. "Reading through tweet histories really can give you a good idea if the person is for real or not. I think that was critical for us getting the interview done," he says.

This anecdote gains even more credibility as the story cites Brian Dresher, manager of social media and digital partnerships at *USA Today*. Dresher agrees that Twitter is a great source for journalists, so much so that he was charged with conducting twice-weekly sessions with the popular newspapers' reporters to teach them how to use that tool.

Both rented social media spaces like Twitter and LinkedIn, as well as your website and blog, are ripe for discoverability. Make those places work for you with great, timely content, and you will be well on your way to being found at just the right time by someone who wants to give you exposure or hire you. Not a bad exchange for going public with your details and providing a clear path to your door.

Own, don't just rent

Online discoverability in today's media environment is controlled largely by four companies: Amazon, Facebook, Google (we'll lump YouTube in with Google, as its owner), and Apple. These companies continue to increase their influence as we expand our use of their products and services. These companies control what results are returned in a search based on their own proprietary algorithms, and as these companies continue to evolve, it is hard to know whether the environment will always be as free as it is today to reach and grow an audience.

Those who are building their micromedia audience on rented space within Facebook, YouTube, or other third-party-controlled channels put themselves at great risk (changes in algorithms or a false copyright charge that shuts down a page, among other risks) over the long term if they don't take ownership over the connection with their audience by converting them to their own list. To prevent any problems in the future, you should be working to move your audience onto channels you control fully so that you continue to own the connection for years to come.

For example, it is terrific to have five thousand contacts on LinkedIn or tens of thousands of Twitter followers but the next step in making your activity in that space truly pay off is to create an incentive for these colleagues, connections, and fans to come with you to your own forum where you can capture their email address or another means of being in touch. This final step is very frequently overlooked. Find a way to create your own list of contacts so you aren't in danger of losing them, and all the work it took to get them interested in your platform in the first place, if the forum you are using suddenly nosedives in popularity, goes under, gets purchased or revamps format in a way that doesn't benefit you. Consider this your "renter's" insurance, if you will, when you participate on any site that you don't own.

Build media strategies across both traditional and virtual platforms

There is a lot of valuable information available on how to navigate the evolving media space. Some of it takes into account what we have carefully outlined in this book as *rented* space (LinkedIn, Facebook, Twitter, Instagram, Snapchat, and other platforms), *owned* space (your website, blog, or any other online space that you create, own, and control completely), and *earned* space (coverage by another outlet that requires the permission of a gatekeeper).

But individual strategies fail to address today's media environment in a few crucial ways. First, they suggest that earned media remains the only way to gain mass exposure. Furthermore, they fail to recognize the way all three areas—earned, owned, and rented—support and feed one another, working in an endless loop. Finally, they lack a clear way to drive an audience to the owned space where it can have lasting power and continue to create value.

As you bring your plan together, think about how what you're doing in one area can be deployed to unlock movement in another, as well as how the skills you are building in one area can work in another.

Don't be distracted by a bit of a turf war that has unfortunately surfaced between public relations professionals as the world around them changes. Those of us in PR are a little weary from a scenario playing out in many businesses today, from small businesses to multinational corporations, where media specialists are hearing the directive "Bring in those digital, social, online specialists to figure out what we do now!" As authors who work on both sides of the mythical divide, we commiserate. As pragmatists, we disagree with the mindset. This may give you confidence, as you begin to realize the talent you have for writing timely blog posts will aid you in constructing the perfect Tweet, which may spark an opportunity for further media attention—all a result of your growing communication savvy and your willingness to consider diving in on whatever new app or platform arrives next that connects with your goal set.

Make a written plan

Just as we have urged you to work backward in other areas of platform building, we suggest you start your media strategy work by envisioning the outcome. Decide exactly what kind of a presence you would like to have before you attempt to create it. If your goal is to have a website that showcases your skills, your blog, your speaking business, and your new book, make that a goal. If in the next calendar year you would like to contribute regularly to the *Huffington Post* and HBR.org, add that to your list. Next, assess your comfort level and participation on existing social media platforms. What two or three sites have you added to your daily routine? Add those to your goal list, with an eye toward becoming more strategic with your activity there, as well as a push to understand how those outlets relate to your other goals, like booking more speeches or becoming a regular contributor. Add, or at least research, another platform and add it to the mix of what you are currently doing. Don't expect to fully understand how to execute on this strategy, but strive to broaden your thinking so that it encompasses content, activity, and effort across all platforms. Write it down. Refer to this document whenever you find yourself trying to do "something" to promote yourself.

Use your common sense, which applies in both the traditional and micromedia worlds. Use the existing tools, whatever those might be at the time you are reading this, and construct a strategy that uses all of them to support and amplify one another. Engage with experts when needed, but vet them to be sure they don't think too narrowly, something usually detectable in their tone and attitude when discussing platforms where they don't have working knowledge or a high level of expertise. We understand that those threatened by extinction with the advent of shiny new toys, now available in the micromedia world, will sneer at them almost reflexively. For your own sake, find someone who can speak intelligently about all media outlets, respects all existing platforms, and can manage them well and in concert.

Aim for accuracy and authenticity everywhere you are

Yes, that's a lot of alliteration, but we waited until nearly the end of the book to use it to avoid alienating anyone annoyed by it! Empires have been built and careers launched by the effective creation, deployment, and management of a false image. Some of those are even based, at least in part, on actual skill, ability, fact, or a truly 100 percent original thought, product, or idea. Many are not. We urge you not to start or continue with any promotional effort based on misconception or lies. At the risk of dispensing moral or spiritual advice, let us say that promoting in a way that is real and genuine, based on education, working knowledge, and experience, will take *less* of a toll than attempting to be something you are not. And that doesn't even get into the serious ethics questions that might haunt you if you find yourself half-heartedly pushing along with a platform that is loosely, but not quite, based on the actual truth. Be who you are. Perhaps even consider being *more* of who you are so that it shows up or reads well in the new and larger public space.

Being real is one thing. Being you with the advice of experts who understand the best parts of your platform and know how to magnify them in a way that produces results is quite another. We live in a do-it-yourself world that has empowered many of us to do things we might not have attempted otherwise. We are in favor of this and the can-do attitude it inspires. But the public space, in almost every case, is really better approached with companions who spend every day immersed in it. They know the jargon, the unspoken rules, even the attitude that varied platforms and media outlets require. Tap them for this expertise. There are too many painful examples of disaster, ranging from disgraced politicians who misunderstood the concept of *public* posts, to sports heroes who went down when they started believing their own hype. Find experts. Hire them. Collaborate with them. And take their advice when you find yourself in unfamiliar waters. In the end, it remains almost humanly impossible to promote yourself or your work in a way that is completely objective.

Create a community to surround your platform

The 1989 film *Field of Dreams,* in which an Iowa corn farmer, played by Kevin Costner, follows the command of voices he hears while working on his land, comes to mind as a good analogy to remember when creating owned media and driving audience there. In the film, Costner's character builds a baseball diamond so that a long-dead, dream team comprised of his late sports idols will arrive to play ball. This gave rise to a popular and often quoted lesson to "build it and they will come." Yes, we know it worked for Costner on the big screen, but its applicability in the micromedia landscape before you is regrettably far less effective. Don't build it and *hope* they will come—build it *so* they will come, and give them a very specific reason to do so.

We wholeheartedly urge you to build a website, start writing a blog, begin participating in social media, and consume traditional media that covers your industry, focuses on thought leaders and experts, or highlights areas of personal interest. All of these activities, in varying degrees and combinations, are very effective means of increasing your visibility or, at the very least, giving you solid knowledge about how to contribute yourself. Notice, too, that they all require some level of commitment, generally either in the labor associated with creation and participation, or in the time required to read, listen, and watch content from others. By all means, start with these activities as you build a platform. But do not stop there.

Once your architecture is in place, replace the list of startup activities with ones that will draw an audience. This task is harder but must be done deliberately, rather than left to fate or chance. We repeat: don't build it and *hope* they will come—build it *so* they will come, and give them a very specific reason to do so. This is an area where, again, you need to become detailed and specific. Creating your platform has ideally equipped you with some very valuable knowledge on what differentiates you from your competitors. Do not assume, as many we cited in the early stages of mastering the new media landscape, that *everyone* is interested in your message, your mission, your project, your service, or your book. You should now know very specifically who in the vast general space is most likely to come into your auditorium and take a seat. Identify those you would like to sign up for your content this year, this week, or in time for that big talk you're giving next month. Have a list of what we call stretch targets, ideal contacts who will visibly ratchet up your reputation and visibility. And finally, don't forget the first adopters. Just as so many people chase that single, elusive, national target and ignore the smaller ones on their path, be very certain your offering does not alienate those who came in the door first and gave you strong indications that your idea was viable.

While there are three specific groups involved in audience building—the legacy or first-in crowd, those whose views or expertise overlap with yours, and those who will require you to fine-tune your offering—all generally respond to the same things. You need something that is irresistible, something that gives them value or knowledge, and a benefit that comes only with signing up to receive your material.

The first two components seem fairly self-explanatory and have already been well explored in this text. Being compelling and bringing new information should, by now, be baked into your efforts to attract attention both online and off. The membership benefit may be the tactic most ripe for creativity. Sample book chapters, coupons, contests, and other free offerings do work, but they are becoming commonplace as well. Consider password-protected areas of a website for members only, or pull together a free offer for a one-on-one session for those who might not be completely convinced about your viewpoint or quite ready to enlist your services. By and large, *engaging* with your new audience often works best. Give people an opportunity to engage with others by way of your special offering. Let them share their own experiences and go even further by inviting them to recognize others—a need that is growing in our increasingly transactional world. Surrounding the release of her remarkable book *One Thousand Gifts*, author Ann Voskamp encouraged her audience to make their own list of #1000Gifts and share the blessings and gifts in their own lives with others online. The campaign was a huge success because it empowered her audience to personalize the message and, in doing so, it launched an extended run on the bestseller list and touched more than a million lives.

PARTING WORDS

For all the speed, change, and nuance in the media landscape as we once knew it, having a voice that reaches an intended audience and changes their lives for the better is still a concept that excites us. From its earliest roots in humanity to its modern equivalent in social media, communication is a lifelong journey for anyone with information to share. We hope we have given you an understandable framework to create a strategy that works for you, some clear guidance that inspires you, and, most of all, a plan for moving the needle that is specifically suited to you and your mission.

We can't wait to see and hear—and read and watch—the results.

NOTES

Introduction

1. Scott Gelber, "The Best Decade Ever? The 1990s, Obviously," *New York Times*, February 8, 2015.
2. Thomas Koulopoulos and Dan Keldsen, *The Gen Z Effect: The Six Forces Shaping the Future of Business* (Bibliomotion, 2014), p. 3.

Chapter 2

1. Judith Newman, "Hung by a Thread," *New York Times*, August 30, 2015.

Chapter 3

1. Andrew Edgecliffe-Johnson, "The Invasion of Corporate News," *Financial Times*, September 19, 2014.
2. Ignite Social Media, "Facebook Brand Pages Suffer 44% Decline in Reach Since December 1," December 10, 2013.

Chapter 4

1. DMR, "By the Numbers: 120 LinkedIn Statistics," February 25, 2015; Pew Research Center, "Demographics of Key Social Networking Platforms," January 9, 2015; TNW, January 29, 2014.
2. Pew Research Center, Journalism and Media, "The Growth in Digital Reporting," March 26, 2014.
3. See onlinenewspapers.com.
4. Reluctant Speakers Club, "Do You Need Emotional Jump Leads to Keep Your Audience Engaged?" July 12, 2012.

Chapter 5
1. Cision, "National Survey Finds Majority of Journalists Now Depend on Social Media for Research," January 20, 2010.

Chapter 7
1. Adweek,"79% of People 18–44 Have Their Smartphones with Them 22 Hours a Day," IDC Research Study, April 2, 2013.
2. HubSpot, "Hubspot State of Inbound 2014."
3. American Press Institute, "How Americans Get Their News," March 13, 2014.

Chapter 9
1. Steve Lohr, "The Age of Big Data," *New York Times*, February 11, 2012.

Chapter 10
1. Pew Research Center, "In Changing News Landscape, Even Television Is Vulnerable: Trends in News Consumption: 1991–2012," September 27, 2012.
2. Kevin Maney, "Think Fast: SmartWatch Slices Thought into Eight-Second Bursts," *Newsweek*, April 18, 2015.
3. Newspaper National Network, "Print Trumps Digital Reading for Many Millennials," February 2014.
4. NBC, "John Oliver Adds Investigative Journalism to His Comedy," September 28, 2014.

Chapter 11
1. CNN, "Obama, Lady Gaga Compete for Facebook Fan Record," June 25, 2010.
2. Mashable, "Ashton Will Hit One Million Fans on Facebook Before Twitter," April 16, 2009.
3. Rob Price, "Inside Ashton Kutcher's Celebrity-Powered Viral Media Empire, Which No One Knows Exists," *Business Insider*, February 19, 2015.
4. James Joyner, "Secrets of Greatness: Practice and Hard Work," Beyond the Beltway, October 25, 2006.
5. Geoff Colvin, "What It Takes to Be Great," *Fortune*, October 19, 2006.

6. Malcolm Gladwell, *Outliers: The Story of Success* (New York: Little, Brown, 2008).
7. Dorie Clark, "How to Become a Professional Speaker," *Forbes*, June 10, 2013.
8. "By the Numbers: 80+ YouTube Facts," *Direct Media Report*, May 23, 2015.
9. Harris Poll, "Face-to-Face Still Tops for Purchase Decisions," July 10, 2009.
10. Celia McGee, "Authors Find New Income as Speakers," *New York Times*, June 4, 2007.

Chapter 12

1. Eric Pfanner, "Peering into the Future of Media," *New York Times*, October 14, 2013.
2. Cision, "National Survey Finds Majority of Journalists Now Depend on Social Media for Research," January 20, 2010.
3. Brenda Ehrlich, "How Journalists Are Using Social Media for Real Results," *Mashable*, April 12, 2010.

ACKNOWLEDGMENTS

Joint Acknowledgments

While we spend our days immersed in publishing, writing a book of our own has been both a challenge and a rare privilege. We'd like to thank the many people who were vital to this project.

To our respective teams at Cave Henricks Communications and Shelton Interactive who were often called to man the front lines during the writing process and contributed their talents to this book's promotion.

To our clients who inspired many of the stories told in these pages.

To Annie Downs, who shared with us her process for turning ideas into legible prose. Armed with poster boards, Post It® notes and Sharpies, her method of charting the course helped us not only divide the labor but kept us from repeating stories, examples, and anecdotes, a particular issue for coauthors.

To early readers Dennis Welch, Michael McDougal, and Nick Alter, who provided crucial outside feedback when the words began to swim on the screen.

To our editors Charlotte Ashlock, Neal Maillet, and Jeevan Sivasubramamian, managing director, Editorial, at Berrett-Koehler, who saw the early potential in this project.

To Maria Jesús Aguiló, Shabnam Banerjee-McFarland, Michael Crowley, Kristen Franz, Katie Sheehan, David Marshall, and Lasell Whipple—the rest of our team at Berrett-Koehler—who guided us so generously and carefully through this process.

Barbara's Acknowledgments

I would like to thank the many people who have supported, guided, and encouraged me over the course of what I call my lucky career, one that has kept me surrounded in big ideas, great books, and the most inspiring, creative minds.

First and foremost, to my husband Michael McDougal, who sat as co-pilot on this book as no one else could have, and who has enriched my life beyond anything I could have hoped for.

Thank you to my eldest daughter Kathryn Leland, whose faith and determination when facing tough odds, in sports and in life, was an incredible example to me when I started a business and began writing this book.

I send much appreciation to my daughter Corinne Julia, whose observant nature taught me the power of listening and watching.

And to my son Brady Nathaniel, whose appetite for adventure has given me a deep appreciation of the world beyond books.

Lynn C. Goldberg has been like a mother, a mentor, and a friend for the past two decades. I am deeply indebted to her for her generous instruction and advice.

My late father, Lloyd L. Cave, instilled in me a deep love for books that lives on today, and my mother, Dolores S. Cave, has provided steady guidance. I am grateful beyond words for my magical, Midwestern childhood.

The Cave Henricks Communications team, past and present, has given me so much more than a chance to launch a business venture. They are colleagues and friends. Thank you to Lewanna Campbell, Dennis Welch, Sara Schneider, Claudia Dizenzo, Jessica Krakoski, Kaila Nickel, Margaret Kingsbury Hansen, Megan Grajeda, and Kimberly Griggs.

An enormous thank-you to my colleague, friend, and now coauthor, Rusty Shelton, who has been a terrific partner on this project and so many others.

Finally, thank you to the many authors and thought leaders who have entrusted me and my company with your great books. We are honored to have been part of the publishing journey.

Rusty Shelton's Acknowledgments

I have been so blessed to receive so much love, wisdom, and support from so many through the years, and it's nice to have a chance to say thank you to a few of them.

I will start by thanking my wife Paige for her love and grace—you're the best wife, mom, and partner I could ever ask for, and I'm so honored to be your husband.

Thanks to Luke and Brady for making me laugh, providing inspiration and perspective, and for adding so much—SO MUCH—fun and meaning to my life. I am proud to be your dad.

I'd like to thank my parents, Walt and Roxanne, for giving so much to me through the years. My dad has always been my role model—what I'm shooting to become—and my mom has always been my rock and biggest fan. Thanks for being the best parents a Texas boy could have ever asked for. You inspired so much confidence in me.

Thanks to my sister Courtney, for being the most courageous woman I know and for providing a great example to me for what a happy and successful life should look like. Thanks to her husband, Chad, who has become like a brother to me.

I'd like to thank my coauthor and good friend Barbara Cave Henricks for being such a fantastic partner on this book.

You have opened many doors for me in my career, and I'm so honored and proud to have coauthored this book with you.

I'd like to thank Charlotte Ashlock and Neal Maillet for seeing the potential in this book and for making it so much better thanks to their wisdom, guidance, and vision throughout the whole process.

Thanks to the entire Berrett-Koehler staff for the hard work, dedication, and wisdom they put into making this book a reality.

Thanks to my mother-in-law, Sharon Naber, and her husband, Brian Naber, for their love, support, and great example; and to my old friends John and Macy Douglas, for whom I'm so happy to be in the same family.

Thanks to the one and only Shelby Sledge for her friendship, wisdom, hard work, and partnership through the years.

Thanks to Amber McGinty, whose counterintuitive spirit and hard work were drivers of so much success for us at Shelton Interactive, for being a wonderful friend.

Thank you to the Shelton Interactive staff—past and present—for making this all possible. I'm honored to work alongside each of you. I am forever grateful to Vanessa Navarro, Tiffany Ballard, Andrea Sanchez, Katie Schnack, Shelby Janner, Brandon Procell, Anthony Aguilar, Wes Fang, Travis Wilson, Sara Pence, Patti Conrad, Melanie Cloth, Paige Velasquez, Paige Dillon, Tiffany Jones, Taylor Ballard, Allison Bright, Whitney Burnett, Katrina Barber, Beth Gwazdosky, David Luna, Lauren King, Richard Ricondo, Will Ruff, Sam Joseph, Marshall Weber, Jeremy Strom, and others.

Thank you to the Shelton Interactive family of clients—each and every one—who have worked with us to start conversations that matter since 2010. You've taught me so much, and I'm forever grateful to you for being part of the SI family.

Thanks to Nick Alter for being such a great friend, partner, and important voice on this book. I'm proud to work with you.

Thanks to my grandmother, Gay Davis, for instilling so much confidence in me and showing so much love to her first grandchild, and my grandfather, Richard "Paw" Grimes, for introducing me to John Wayne and fishing and for making his first grandchild feel like the king of the world.

Thanks to my grandmother, Tyler Rose Queen Catherine "Granny" Shelton, for her love, and my grandfather, Jerry "Grandaddy" Shelton, for helping me appreciate the game of golf and providing such a great example of relationship building and business success.

Thanks to my uncle Rusty for setting such a wonderful example and for going out of his way to be a true mentor to me through the years, and to my aunt Julia for her love and support.

Thanks to my uncle Dick for teaching me so much about building relationships and providing an example of how to succeed at sales and marketing while still being true to your word during those summers we ran cars together, and to his wife Debbie, for whom I'm so thankful.

Thanks to my uncle Randy for providing such a great example of resilience and aunt Lydia for her example of grace and love.

I have been blessed with many mentors through the years.

Thanks to Clint Greenleaf for showing me what a true entrepreneur looks like and for giving the gift of his time, wisdom, and connections to set me up for success while I launched and grew Shelton Interactive.

Thanks to Robbie Vorhaus, who counseled me through plenty of tough times, gave me the benefit of his experience and relationships, and who shares a vision with me for what a modern MarCom Agency should look like.

Mike Odom taught me so much of what I know about sales and marketing. He and Steve Joiner took a chance on me right out of college and gave me far more time and training than they ever needed to. For that wisdom, time, and the opportunity they gave me, I'll be forever grateful.

Thanks to Dr. Jeff Brown for the writing tips, media training, and friendship through the years. You're the best.

Thanks to William J. Rouhana and Amy Newmark for giving me a shot back in 2008 and for offering wisdom, experience, and friendship through the years.

I have had so many people open so many doors for me in my professional career, and I'd like to thank Dr. Julie Silver, Lisa Tener, Erika Heilman, Jill Friedlander, Carolyn Monaco, Heather Adams, Curtis Yates, Lee Hough (whom I miss), Dr. Richard Senelick, Michael Larsen, Elizabeth Pomada, Matt Bialer, James Levine, Joelle Jarvis, and many others.

I have so many friends to thank for their support through the years, including Evan and Courtney Epstein, Logan and Hayley Kimble, John and Lisa Hale, Troy Knight, Ryan and Jazmyn Lynch, Sean and Britania O'Brien, Michael Felan, Justin and Jennifer Sander, Zak and Stacy Sage, Michael and Sarah Hoffman, Ben and Shannon De Leon, Michael and Thao Swimelar, Joel and Beth Mayor, Dax and Cameron Williamson, Johnny and Jessica Powis, Sam and Lindsay Rhodes, Cale and Dorene Stubbe, Soren and DeeAnn Bredgaard, Dale Griffin, Alwyne McDonald, Nick Bloomingdale, Andy Lyons, Robert Warren, JT and Angela Hearn, and countless others.

I'd like to thank Adam Witty, Jenn Ash, and the fabulous team at Advantage Media Group for their support, encouragement, and partnership.

Thanks to my EO Forum (13X!) for their friendship and consistent example of what success looks like. They include Kim Overton, Shauna Martin, John Carter, David Osborne, Michael Dadashi, Jason Crabtree, Chris Gober, and Natalie Kennedy.

Thanks to my church family at Highland Park in Austin for providing the foundation and support that made me believe I could achieve whatever I wanted to.

INDEX

ABOUT THE AUTHORS

BARBARA CAVE HENRICKS is president of Cave Henricks Communications, a full-service public relations firm specifically created for books, authors, and thought leaders.

A former journalist at NBC Radio, Barbara moved to Manhattan and into publishing in 1989, landing a position in the publicity department at Workman, a publisher that grew to fame with its innovative packaging and design. She then spent six years at Houghton Mifflin as the associate director of publicity, handling a prestigious list of nonfiction titles by authors such as Vice President Al Gore, astronaut James Lovell, Pulitzer Prize winners Tracy Kidder and Buzz Bissinger, poet Diane Ackerman, and novelists Ethan Canin and Amy Ephron. In 1996, she joined Goldberg McDuffie Communications and in 2000, helped create and lead the company's division, Goldberg McDuffie Business, where she served as vice president.

In 2007, Barbara opened her own firm, which represents about twenty-five titles and authors a year, working with bestsellers and thought leaders around the globe. The company has notably launched popular titles such as *StrengthsFinder 2.0* by Tom Rath, *The One Thing* by Gary Keller and Jay Papasan,

Global Tilt by Ram Charan, and *Humans Are Underrated* by Geoff Colvin.

Barbara has spearheaded campaigns for some of the biggest names in business, including Jack Welch (*Jack: Straight from the Gut*), Larry Bossidy, Ram Charan (*Execution* and *Confronting Reality*), Vanguard founder John Bogle (*The Battle for the Soul of Capitalism*), Marcus Buckingham (*First, Break All the Rules*), Maria Bartiromo (*Use the News*), and Clay Christensen (*The Innovator's DNA*).

Barbara speaks and presents on the media and public relations at events around the country, including the Texas Writers Conference, the 800 CEO Read Author Pow-Wow, the Soundview Executive Book Summit, and, notably in 2012, with Rusty Shelton, at SXSW Interactive. She has been featured in *Publishers Weekly*, *The Atlantic*, the *New York Sun* and on several radio stations around the country.

A graduate of Indiana University, she lives in Austin, Texas, with her husband, artist Michael McDougal, and three children. This is her first book.

You can learn about speaking and read Barbara's blog at www.barbarahenricks.com or www.cavehenricks.com. You can also connect with her on Twitter (@BarbaraHenricks) or Linked In (www.linkedin.com/pub/barbara-cave-henricks).

RUSTY SHELTON first spoke at Harvard on the changing world of PR and marketing at the age of twenty-three and is an active keynote speaker on marketing, social media, and the evolving media landscape.

Rusty founded Shelton Interactive in 2010, and it has gone on to become one of the country's fastest-growing brand communications agencies. Shelton Interactive features a unique and forward-thinking model that integrates PR, social media, graphic design, website development, and search engine optimization—services that are normally handled by multiple agencies—under one roof for more efficient and effective campaigns.

In addition to working with leading businesses and brands —including Chicken Soup for the Soul, Russell Stover, Kellogg School of Management, and Harvard Medical School—Shelton Interactive has led campaigns for some of the biggest best-sellers of the past few years, including *The One Thing* by Gary Keller and Jay Papasan, *The Confidence Code* by Claire Shipman and Katty Kay, *One Thousand Gifts* by Ann Voskamp, *Take the Stairs* by Rory Vaden, *How the World Sees You* by Sally Hogshead, *Eat Move Sleep* by Tom Rath, *Do Over* by Jon Acuff, and many others.

An NSA speaker, Rusty speaks regularly on the changing media landscape, including SXSW Interactive and Harvard Medical School's CME Publishing and Leadership Course.

An avid Texas Longhorns fan, Rusty sits on the University of Texas Texas Exes PR Committee and is also a proud member of Entrepreneurs' Organization (EO) in Austin.

He lives just west of Austin in the Texas Hill Country town of Spicewood with his wife, Paige; two sons, Luke and Brady, and a new daughter; and their very rowdy black lab, Charlie.

You can access resources and learn more about keynote and workshop opportunities at www.RustyShelton.com or www.SheltonInteractive.com. You can also connect with him on Twitter (@RustyShelton), Instagram (www.Instagram.com/RustyRShelton), or LinkedIn (www.linkedin.com/in/RustyR Shelton).

Berrett–Koehler
Publishers

Berrett-Koehler is an independent publisher dedicated to an ambitious mission: *connecting people and ideas to create a world that works for all.*

We believe that to truly create a better world, action is needed at all levels—individual, organizational, and societal. At the individual level, our publications help people align their lives with their values and with their aspirations for a better world. At the organizational level, our publications promote progressive leadership and management practices, socially responsible approaches to business, and humane and effective organizations. At the societal level, our publications advance social and economic justice, shared prosperity, sustainability, and new solutions to national and global issues.

A major theme of our publications is "Opening Up New Space." Berrett-Koehler titles challenge conventional thinking, introduce new ideas, and foster positive change. Their common quest is changing the underlying beliefs, mindsets, institutions, and structures that keep generating the same cycles of problems, no matter who our leaders are or what improvement programs we adopt.

We strive to practice what we preach—to operate our publishing company in line with the ideas in our books. At the core of our approach is stewardship, which we define as a deep sense of responsibility to administer the company for the benefit of all of our "stakeholder" groups: authors, customers, employees, investors, service providers, and the communities and environment around us.

We are grateful to the thousands of readers, authors, and other friends of the company who consider themselves to be part of the "BK Community." We hope that you, too, will join us in our mission.

A BK Business Book

This book is part of our BK Business series. BK Business titles pioneer new and progressive leadership and management practices in all types of public, private, and nonprofit organizations. They promote socially responsible approaches to business, innovative organizational change methods, and more humane and effective organizations.

Berrett–Koehler
Publishers

Connecting people and ideas
to create a world that works for all

Dear Reader,

Thank you for picking up this book and joining our worldwide community of Berrett-Koehler readers. We share ideas that bring positive change into people's lives, organizations, and society.

To welcome you, we'd like to offer you a free e-book. You can pick from among twelve of our bestselling books by entering the promotional code **BKP92E** here: http://www.bkconnection.com/welcome.

When you claim your free e-book, we'll also send you a copy of our e-newsletter, the *BK Communiqué*. Although you're free to unsubscribe, there are many benefits to sticking around. In every issue of our newsletter you'll find

• A free e-book
• Tips from famous authors
• Discounts on spotlight titles
• Hilarious insider publishing news
• A chance to win a prize for answering a riddle

Best of all, our readers tell us, "Your newsletter is the only one I actually read." So claim your gift today, and please stay in touch!

Sincerely,

Charlotte Ashlock
Steward of the BK Website

Questions? Comments? Contact me at bkcommunity@bkpub.com.

Certified

Corporation
bcorporation.net